Vladimir Lenin, Joseph Stalin & Leon Trotsky: The Soviet Union's Big Three

By Charles River Editors

About Charles River Editors

Charles River Editors was founded by Harvard and MIT alumni to provide superior editing and original writing services, with the expertise to create digital content for publishers across a vast range of subject matter. In addition to providing original digital content for third party publishers, Charles River Editors republishes civilization's greatest literary works, bringing them to a new generation via ebooks.

Introduction

Vladimir Lenin (1870-1924)

"We want to achieve a new and better order of society: in this new and better society there must be neither rich nor poor; all will have to work. Not a handful of rich people, but all the working people must enjoy the fruits of their common labour." – Vladimir Lenin

Among the leaders of the 20th century, arguably none shaped the course of history as much as Vladimir Lenin (1870-1942), the Communist revolutionary and political theorist who led the Bolshevik Revolution that established the Soviet Union. In addition to shaping the Marxist-Leninist political thought that steered Soviet ideology, he was the first Soviet premier until his death and set the Soviet Union on its way to becoming one of the world's two superpowers for most of the century, in addition to being the West's Cold War adversary.

Given the Red Scare and the nature of the Cold War, Lenin has always been a divisive and controversial figure in Western society, especially among those who equate the Soviets with brutal repression and human rights abuses. Lenin also has his champions, who point to the fact that he got Russia out of World War I, was the first to successfully implement a modern socialist state, and worked tirelessly to elevate the working classes.

As it turned out, the creation of the Soviet Union came near the end of Lenin's life, as he worked so hard that he had burned himself out by his 50s, dying in 1924 after a series of strokes had completely debilitated him. Since his life before the Soviet Union naturally gets less focus, Lenin remains a bit of an unknown among many, and he is likely a lesser known or notorious figure than his successor, Joseph Stalin. *The Soviet Union's Big Three* explores Lenin's life and work before the Bolshevik Revolution, as well as the crucial role he played in establishing the Soviet Union. Along with pictures of important people, places, and events, you will learn about the founder of Communist Russia like you never have before.

Joseph Stalin (1878-1953)

"It is time to finish retreating. Not one step back! Such should now be our main slogan." – Joseph Stalin

If Adolf Hitler had not inflicted the devastation of World War II upon Europe, it's quite likely that the West would consider Joseph Stalin (1878-1953) the 20th century's greatest tyrant. A Bolshevik revolutionary who played a crucial role in the Russian Revolution of 1917 and the establishment of the Soviet Union, Stalin was one of the Communist regime's earliest leaders and went about consolidating power after the death of Vladimir Lenin, whose final wishes were that Stalin be removed from his post as General Secretary of the Communist Party and not be given the ability to take power.

Of course, Stalin managed to do just that, modernizing the Soviet Union at a breakneck pace on the backs of millions of poor laborers and prisoners. Before World War II, Stalin consolidated his position by frequently purging party leaders (most famously Leon Trotsky) and Red Army leaders, executing hundreds of thousands of people at the least. In one of history's greatest textbook examples of the idea that the enemy of my enemy is my friend, Stalin's Soviet Union allied with Britain and the United States to defeat Hitler in Europe, with the worst of the war's carnage coming on the eastern front during Germany's invasion of Russia. Nevertheless, the victory in World War II established the Soviet Union as of the world's two superpowers for nearly 50 years, in addition to being the West's Cold War adversary.

By the time Stalin died in 1953, it was written that he "had found Russia working with wooden ploughs and [is] leaving it equipped with atomic piles." Of course, he was reviled in the West, where it was written, "The names of Lenin, Stalin, and Hitler will forever be linked to the tragic course of European history in the first half of the twentieth century." *The Soviet Union's Big Three* explores Stalin's life and work before the Bolshevik Revolution, as well as the crucial role he played in establishing the Soviet Union and turning it into a modern superpower. Along with pictures of important people, places, and events, you will learn about Stalin like you never have before.

Leon Trotsky (1879-1940)

"Stalin, aware of the state of his regime and in what a tottering world he lived, did not count Trotsky's meagre following and then sit back in comfort. He knew that as long as Trotsky lived and could write and speak, the Soviet bureaucracy was in mortal danger. In a conversation just before war broke out, Hitler and the French ambassador discussed the perils of plunging Europe into conflict and agreed that the winner of the second great war might be Trotsky. Winston Churchill hated him with a personal malevolence which seemed to overstep the bounds of reason. These men knew his stature, the power of what he stood for, and were never lulled by the smallness of his forces." – C.L.R. James, 1940

A lot of ink has been spilled covering the lives of history's most influential figures, but how much of the forest is lost for the trees? In Charles River Editors' Russian Legends series, readers can get caught up to speed on the lives of Russia's most important men and women in the time it takes to finish a commute, while learning interesting facts long forgotten or never known.

For much of the 20th century, the struggle between capitalism and communism was one of the central dramas, and the figure of Leon Trotsky stood for many on the political left as a reminder of a road not taken. Along with Vladimir Lenin, Trotsky led the October Bolshevik Revolution of 1917 and held crucial posts in the early Soviet governments, but after Lenin's death Trotsky was exiled, persecuted and finally murdered at the behest of his arch-rival, Joseph Stalin. For the final decade of his life, Trotsky was a man trapped in between two worlds. A communist seeking refuge in the capitalist West, Trotsky was deemed a secret agent of the capitalist powers by Stalin's propaganda, but the Soviet Union's enemies also viewed him with suspicion.

In the initial aftermath of Lenin's death, Trotsky had been his ally's heir apparent, and for those inclined to believe the Soviet experiment had started promisingly but gone astray, Trotsky became the embodiment of the betrayed promise of the early Bolshevik revolution. There were certain ironies in this widespread sympathetic interpretation of Trotsky's legacy. For the Marxists and Marxist sympathizers appalled by Stalin's paranoid police state, Gulag concentration camps, and strict suppression of dissent, Trotsky was viewed as a humane and cosmopolitan opposite to Stalin. But Trotsky himself had overseen and spearheaded campaigns of persecution against Russians suspected of "counterrevolutionary" leanings, and he had written a long tract defending these "terroristic" measures as necessary safeguards of the revolution. Other sympathetic observers asserted that while Stalin took refuge in a chauvinistic Russian nationalism, Trotsky's political goals were always international in scope, but Trotsky's internationalist perspective envisioned a state of cataclysmic international conflict on a global scale as a necessary precursor to the victory of communism.

One reason Trotsky is remembered so differently is that he had a greater intellectual and cultural sophistication than Stalin, including a positive disposal toward the avant-garde movements of the 20th century arts and a strong interest in Einstein's physics and Freud's psychoanalysis. In the early post-revolutionary Soviet Union, avant-garde art, literature, and cinema flourished, but under Stalin artists were obliged to hew to the tenets of "socialist realism," which in practice often let to kitschy, idealized paintings and films celebrating collective farm workers operating tractors and combine harvesters. Ultimately, Stalin's mastery of propaganda and his willingness to tap into traditional Russian mythologies of religious nationalism keyed his political success, while Trotsky's more cosmopolitan refinement and sympathy for "Western" artistic and intellectual trends lent itself to insinuations that he was a Western capitalist sleeper agent and something less than a true Russian. Trotsky's Jewish origins provided further cause for suspicion among Russian nationalists.

The Soviet Union's Big Three explores Trotsky's life and work before the Bolshevik Revolution, as well as the crucial role he played in establishing the Soviet Union and his rivalry with Stalin. Along with pictures of important people, places, and events, you will learn about Trotsky like never before.

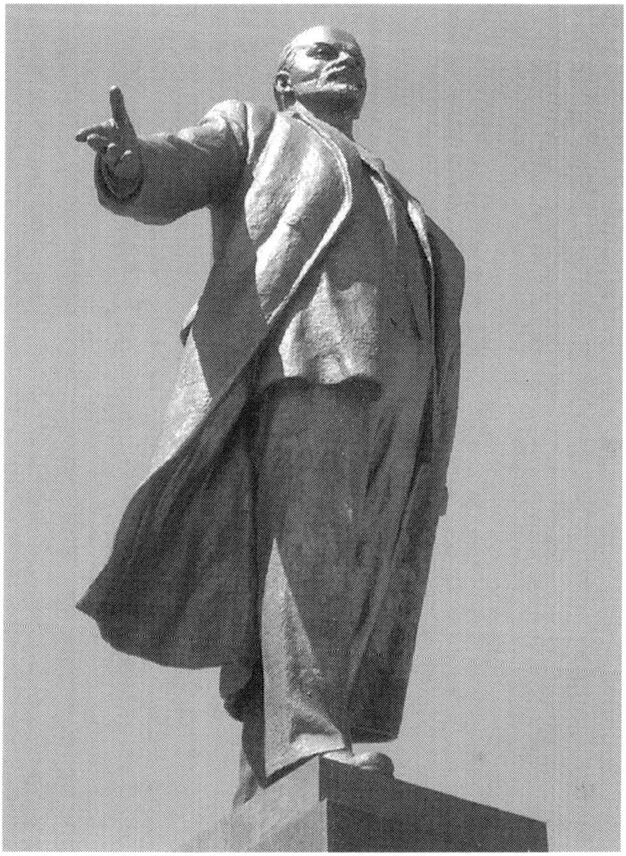

Chapter 1: Lenin's Early Years

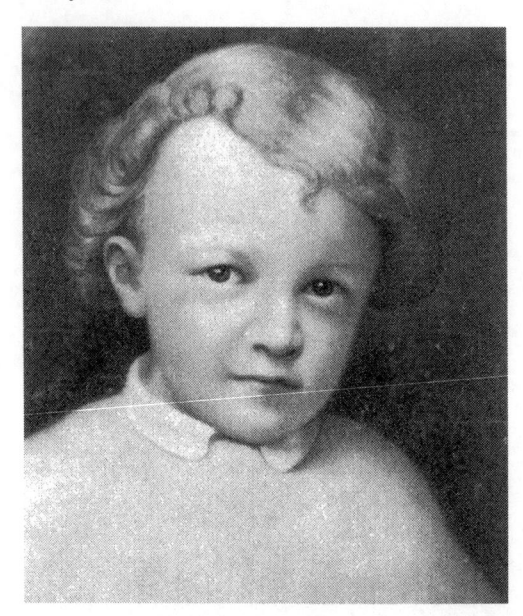

4 year old Lenin

On April 10, 1870, the founder of Russian Communism was born Vladimir Illich Ulyanov to parents Ilya and Maria, who were middle class citizens of the small town of Simbirsk in Russia. Vladimir was their third child, joining Anna and Alexander, and over the next several years, there would be more siblings: Olga, Nikolai, Dmitry and Mariya. With the exception of Nikolai, who died shortly after birth, all his siblings would contribute in some way to the shaping of Lenin's political convictions.

In Lenin's father, we see the first of many ironies that plagued him throughout his life. Though he had hailed from a poor peasant background, Ilya had degrees in both physics and mathematics from the University of Kazan and had taught both at the Penza Institute for the Nobility. By the time "Volodya" (as little Vladimir was known to his family) was born, Ilya had been made the Director of Public Schools for the entire province. During his career, Ilya would supervise the construction of more than 450 schools, built during Russia's 19th century era of modernization, and in recognition of his hard work and success, the Tsar awarded him the Order of St. Vladimir and the position of a hereditary nobleman. Thus, Ilya did what Vladimir would later claim was impossible in Russia: raised himself through ambition and hard work from a peasant to a nobleman. In fact, had there been no revolution, Lenin himself would have inherited his father's title and could have lived out his life as one of the very noblemen whom he had imprisoned and killed.

Ilya

Maria was also well read and well educated. The daughter of a doctor, she grew up in a wealthy family where learning was emphasized for everyone, even the women. She was taught at home by excellent tutors and showed a particular interest in languages and Russian literature. She had a teaching certificate but did not use it after marrying Ilya, though by that time she was fluent in English, French, German, and Russian.

One of the areas of life on which the couple disagreed was religion. Ilya was a member of the Russian Orthodox Church and was very devout, insisting that all his children be baptized and raised in that faith. Maria, on the other hand, was from a Lutheran background and had no particular interest in religion one way or another. It appears that it was her influence, at least in part, that led Lenin towards eventual atheism.

Before then, though, the Ulyanov children would lead relatively happy, well cared-for lives. Their parents were politically neutral, so there was never any threat from the government. Their father went about his work every day while the children went to school at the Simbirsk Gymnasium and Maria cared for the home. The family spent most evenings around the fireplace or dining room table, where Ilya saw to it that his children studied hard so that they would always be star pupils in the schools he supervised. This suited Vladimir just fine, as he was an excellent student and would spend much of his teen years tutoring both his siblings and others in Latin.

The Ulyanovs spent much of their summers with their cousins on Maria's side of the family in a rambling old manor house in Kokushkino. There Vladimir always had someone to play with, whether it was his little sister Olga, with whom he was particularly close, or one of his cousins. On nice days the children tended to play outdoors, retiring when they were tired to rest with a few games of chess.

Sadly, all this came to an end in 1886 when Ilya died of a sudden brain aneurism, when Lenin was just 16. It was around this time that the teenaged Vladimir became an open and avowed atheist. Meanwhile, left a widow with four children still at home, Maria was forced to sell some of the family's property to make ends meet, and to keep her oldest son, Alexander, at St. Petersburg University where he was studying biology. Unfortunately, Alexander might have been better off if he'd had to drop out.

A bright student with a sharp mind, Alexander was not just studying biology; he was also dabbling in ant-Tsarist politics. His favorite authors, Nikolay Chernyshevsky, Dmitry Pisarev and Karl Marx, were all banned on campus because of their diatribes against absolute monarchy. In addition to reading them himself, Alexander also passed these books on to his younger brother, who devoured them with fascination. Vladimir particularly liked Chernyshevsky's *What is to be Done?*

Unfortunately, Alexander and his friends in the People's Will on the university campus were doing more than reading. By 1886 they had decided to take matters into their own hands and attempt to overthrow the government by force. Their first step was to assassinate Tsar Alexander III. As the biology student and nominal scientist in the group, it fell to him to construct a bomb they planned to use to blow up the unpopular monarch. However, their plot was unraveled by authorities, and Alexander was hanged on May 8, 1887.

Vladimir in 1887

The quick deaths in succession of his father and brother made Vladimir the head of the family, but Maria was still determined that he complete his University Education, and Vladimir was happy to comply. After graduating with a gold medal for outstanding performance, he applied to study law at his father's alma mater, Kazan University. At first it seemed that he would not be accepted due to his fraternal connection with an executed political criminal, but some men who had known and respected his father intervened, and young Vladimir was accepted in the fall of 1887.

Perhaps to save money, and perhaps hoping to ensure her second son avoided his brother's fate, Maria rented out the family home in Simbirsk and moved in with Vladimir in Kazan. Of course, this begs the question as to what happened to her three younger children during this time. While that remains unclear, it is likely that as a still-young widow Maria turned to her family for help and sent the children to live with relatives.

Maria

Unfortunately, Maria had good reason to be concerned about Vladimir's politics. Soon after starting his studies in Kazan, Lenin joined the Samara-Simbirsk Council, a banned organization on campus. Nevertheless, the group met in secret, and Vladimir rose quickly among its ranks and was chosen to represent the group at the Zemlyachestvo Council, a left-wing organization intent on bringing back the People's Freedom Party (which had assassinated Tsar Alexander II in 1881). On December 4, 1887, he was arrested during a demonstration and expelled from college. In addition, the Ministry of Internal Affairs ordered that he be sent to Maria's family's home in Kokushkino, where they would continue to monitor his behavior.

However, being banished to a quiet country estate only gave Lenin more time to devote to his increasingly radical thinking. Though it remains unclear how he got the books so far from a large city, he read for hours each day, pouring over every belligerent anti-government tome he could get his hands on. Maria was obviously worried about his illegal pursuits and even went as far as to contact the Interior Minister in 1888 to ask that her son be allowed to leave the country and study elsewhere. Though the Minister was not willing to grant the young hot head that level of freedom, he did agree to allow Lenin to return to Kazan to live with Maria and his younger brother Dmitry in a small house on the Pervaya Gora.

Since birds of a feather tend to flock together, Lenin soon made the acquaintance of a fellow revolutionary, M. P. Chetvergova. She was the lynchpin of a secret circle that was devoted to the study and discussion of the works of Karl Marx. Lenin soon became fascinated with Marxist thought, particularly Marx's seminal *Das Kapital*, in which Marx put forth the idea that capitalism is based on the exploitation of the labor of underpaid workers by the owners of the resources they work on. While the young teen had already been dabbling in revolutionary ideals, Marxism really resonated with Lenin, and he became more and more enmeshed in the plight of the workers against the bourgeoisies.

Marx

Maria, herself a member of the bourgeois that her son was condemning, became more and more concerned. In the hopes of getting him away from the influence of his radical friends, she bought a large country house in Alakaevka, Samara Oblast, where she encouraged her son to become a gentleman farmer and to oversee the surrounding gardens and crops. Instead, Lenin spent his time talking to the peasants and studying their way of life. He became increasingly convinced that they were being oppressed by the local landed gentry, and that their poverty could only be alleviated by a radical change in the social and political structure of Russia.

As winter approached that year, Maria moved the family to Samara, a warmer climate where they would not have to deal with the harshest aspects of the notorious Russian winter. Here Vladimir met A. P. Skylyarenko, a dissident who ran a discussion circle devoted to studying and criticizing the government. Together they committed their lives to the propagation of Marxism in their country and the world.

An excellent scholar who had apparently inherited his mother's gift for languages, Lenin spent much of that winter translating Marx and Friedrich Engels's *The Communist Manifesto* from the original German into Russian. He also studied Georgi Plekhanov, who had founded the Black Repartition movement in 1879. Plekhanov maintained that Russia was at that time entering a period of transition in which it would move from being a feudal system to capitalism. This of course disturbed a Marxist like Lenin, since he saw capitalism as the root of all evil.

Engels

Though Maria understandably worried that Vladimir would suffer the same fate as his older brother, one thing that set Lenin and his friends apart from many other radicals of their time (including his deceased brother) was his belief that random violence and murdering officials was pretty useless in the cause of freedom. When he ran into M.V. Sabunaev in 1889, the two shared several heated arguments over her plans to recruit more members to the People Freedom Party in the hopes that they could disrupt the country with random acts of violence. Nearly 15 years later, Lenin would categorically reject the use of "terror", which he described as "the system of individual political assassinations, as being a method of political struggle which is most inexpedient at the present time, diverting the best forces from the urgent and imperatively necessary work of organization and agitation, destroying contact between the revolutionaries and the masses of the revolutionary classes of the population, and spreading both among the revolutionaries themselves and the population in general utterly distorted ideas of the aims and methods of struggle against the autocracy.

Though he did not appear to be following his brother's path of violence against the government, Maria remained concerned enough about Lenin's activities in 1890 that she persuaded the Russian educational authorities to let her son complete his exams for his college degree. After a few months of study, Lenin graduated from the University of Saint Petersburg with highest honors. However, his family's happiness at this triumph was short lived as word soon arrived that his beloved sister Olga had died of typhoid while he was there. For the rest of his life, Lenin would refer affectionately to the little sister he had bullied into following his every command.

Chapter 2: Stalin's Early Years

Stalin's birth house in Gori, Georgia, within the shrine complex built over it in the 1930s. Today it is a museum.

Ioseb Besarionis dze Jughashvili was born the fourth child of Ketevan and Besarion Jughashvili on December 21, 1879. Though his parents were poor peasants living in Gori, Georgia, he was nonetheless pampered and sheltered during his youth, due to the death in infancy of his three older siblings. By the time he was born, his mother was determined not to lose another child to the grim reaper, so she watched his health carefully and made sure he had the best care she and his father, a boot maker, could provide. She even took up washing in order to have more money to provide better food and clothing for her son.

Ketevan

Besarion

Despite his parents' best efforts, young Joseph suffered health scares in childhood. At the age of seven, Joseph experienced the first major health crisis of his life when he came down with smallpox. Night after night his mother sat by his bedside, bathing his feverish head with cool water and trying to keep him from scratching the virulent pox that covered his little body. While little Joseph did survive the dreaded illness, he was left with permanent scars all over his tiny face. For the rest of his childhood he would be taunted by his young friends with the cruel nickname "pocky." One of the most famous aspects of Stalin's regime was its willingness to doctor photos for political purposes, and that extended to Stalin's personal appearance itself, as he later had photographs altered to make his pockmarks less noticeable. Despite being merely 5'4, Stalin would ensure that he was depicted majestically and appear larger than the "little squirt" President Harry S. Truman would later describe upon meeting him.

In addition to that major health scare, young Joseph had a turbulent first 10 years as a result of his father's failed business. Though they were initially faring well, Besarion became an alcoholic and abused his wife and son. Furthermore, the family moved several times during the first decade of Joseph's life, and the young kid grew up in destitute, tough neighborhoods. Even as a child, Joseph engaged in brawls with other kids, experiences that undoubtedly toughened the man who would later famously state, "Gratitude is a sickness suffered by dogs."

In gratitude for his survival of smallpox, the devoutly Christian Ketevan decided her little boy had to have a religious education. She scrimped, saved and wrangled until she secured him a place in the little school run by their local church in 1888. This enraged Besarion, who wished to have the young kid trained as a cobbler. After one drunken episode in which he assaulted Gori's police chief and smashed the windows of the local tavern, Besarion was ordered to leave town. He did so without his family, leaving Ketevan and Joseph on their own.

While at school, the spoiled little boy had his first experience with order and discipline, including having to speak Russian in the classroom instead of his native Georgian. Nevertheless, he excelled in studies, as well as becoming so accomplished at singing that he often sang at weddings.

Although Joseph was excelling in school, he continued to suffer health problems. By the time he started his schooling, Stalin had suffered an injury to his left arm, brought about possibly by blood poisoning or physical abuse, that left his left arm a couple of inches shorter than his right arm. Though Stalin later gave conflicting accounts of how it happened, it was serious enough to exempt him from military service in World War I.

Then, in 1890, Joseph had his second brush with death when he was run over by a carriage pulled by two large horses. While there was no internal damage, his left arm was severely injured and for a time it seemed he might even lose it. With his mother's careful nursing over a period of months, his arm finally healed, but the care available in their small village was not the same as was available in larger cities, so Joseph was sent to convalesce at Tiflis, which just so happened to be the town Stalin's father had headed to after being ordered out of Gori. As a result, his father all but kidnapped the child and forced him to work as a cobbler, only to have Ketevan and Gori's religious authorities track Joseph down and take him back. After that, Besarion would never associate with Joseph or his mother again.

Stalin as a teenager

Because he had always been physically weak, Joseph was accustomed to hours of quiet reading and did well at school, earning a scholarship to the exclusive Tiflis Theological Seminary at the age of 16. While there, Joseph joined Messame Dassy, a secret organization committed to promoting independence for Georgia, and there were also young followers of Karl Marx in the group. This proved to be Stalin's first encounter with the revolutionary socialist ideas brewing in Russia at that time. Stalin continued to read all kinds of literature that had been forbidden, from Victor Hugo's novels to socialist revolutionary material, and he persisted even after being caught and punished on several occasions.

Tiflis Orthodox Theological Seminary, circa 1919

By the time he had completed his first year at the school, Stalin had become an avowed atheist. According to one contemporary, upon reading Darwin's *The Origin of Species*, Stalin remarked, "God's not unjust, he doesn't actually exist. We've been deceived. If God existed, he'd have made the world more just... I'll lend you a book and you'll see."

Four years later, at the age of 20, Stalin was expelled from Tiflis for failure to pay his tuition. However, he had already been in trouble with his superiors for flaunting authority and reading prohibited writings. In fact, the real reason for his dismissal may have been that Stalin was already developing his later legendary leadership skills and had been trying to convert some of his fellow students to Marxist socialism. During his school years, he had insisted that his peers refer to him as "Koba", a Robin Hood like protagonist in Alexander Kazbegi's *The Patricide*, and around the time he left school, Stalin discovered some of the early writings of Vladimir Lenin.

The young student now wished to become a revolutionary.

Chapter 3: Trotsky's Early Years

"Bureaucracy and social harmony are inversely proportional to each other." – Leon Trotsky

A number of the influential 20th century Communist revolutionaries shared the trait of being publicly known and known to posterity mainly by their pseudonyms. Perhaps the most famous example is Ernesto Guevara de la Serna, the glamorous guerrilla who is known to most as Che Guevara, a nickname that initially referred to his status as an Argentine among Cubans ("Che" is popular slang for an Argentine). The "Big Three" of the Russian Revolution are also remembered by names originally adopted when they were clandestine revolutionaries: Vladimir Ilyich Ulyanov became Lenin, apparently after the Lena River; Joseph Vissarionovich Dzugashvilii became Stalin, "the man of steel"; and Lev Davidovich Bronshtein became Trotsky.

8 year old Lev

Trotsky was apparently the surname of a jailer during Lev's early stint as a political prisoner. Bronshtein had written articles under several different pseudonyms when he was an exiled radical, but Trotsky was the name that stuck. Today, his real name is barely remembered.

His parents, David and Anna, were prosperous Jewish farmers in a rural region of what is now the Ukraine. They were assimilated Jews in the sense that they spoke Russian and Ukrainian at home, and they were largely unobservant when it came to religious practice. Assimilation could only go so far, however; the Tsarist governments varied in the degree of persecution and hostility they directed toward Jews in their territories, but the threat of pogroms was never far away.

In the wake of the assassination of Tsar Alexander II in 1881, falsely blamed on Jews, there were massacres of Jewish populations with tacit or explicit government encouragement throughout Russia and the Ukraine. This was the first decade of Trotsky's life, so it's safe to assume that it left some impression on him. Given the pogroms, it is not surprising that many Jews of Trotsky's generation became involved in anti-Tsarist revolutionary movements. Moreover, they had little attachment to the old Russian order, which was founded on a xenophobic religious nationalism that frequently singled out Jews for both violent attacks and legal harassment. The Bronshteins, however, were comfortable and politically uninvolved, and it is not clear to what degree their son's political ideology had developed when he left home for the city of Odessa.

Tsar Alexander II

In Odessa, Lev Davidovich lived with members of his mother's family, people of cosmopolitan and liberal leanings. There he attended a school that had been modeled on the German *Gymnasium* (for more Western-oriented Russians of the period, German models of education, science, and intellectual life were influential). A major port on the Black Sea and the fourth largest city in the Russian Empire, Odessa was an unusually international city with an openness to the world unusual in the more interior regions of the Empire. Its population included Jews, Armenians, Georgians, Persians, Arabs, Greeks, and Italians, along with French, German, and English merchants. At times, the merchants and Jews comprised a third of the total population. For a revolutionary leader who would later become a tireless international traveler (though not always by choice), a veteran of exile, and an advocate of internationalism, Odessa was an understandably formative environment for a teenager. Odessa was also home to a large urban working class receptive to radical political movements, and it subsequently became legendary because of a workers' and sailors' revolt in support of the Revolution of 1905. The rebels were massacred by Tsarist forces in an incident later made famous in revolutionary director Sergei Eisenstein's 1925 film *The Battleship Potemkin*.

In 1896, Lev moved to the city of Nikolayev, another Black Sea port and major shipbuilding center, to continue his education. It was in this center of both student and working class radicalism that he first became immersed in the political ferment of the period. His first affiliations seem to have been with the Narodnik movement, a highly influential local Russian variety of revolutionary populism. The Narodniks idealized the Russian peasant class as the key to political revolution in Russia. They believed that traditional social life in the Russian countryside and village had been essentially communalistic in orientation, and that the Russian path toward socialism lay in awakening the poor rural masses as a revolutionary class to overthrow the Tsarist order.

The Narodniks' most spectacular achievement was the assassination of Tsar Alexander II in 1881, but their success also led to a major campaign of police repression and censorship that weakened the movement. At the same time, the Narodniks had little success in generating popular support among the population they hoped would spearhead the general revolt against Tsarism, due in large part to the fact they were mainly urban middle-class and upper-class students,.

Lev in 1897

Given his Jewish origins and his many years spent in the urban and cosmopolitan Odessa, it is not surprising that Lev would ultimately be drawn away from Narodnism and toward Marxism. Marxism was an ideology of international orientation premised on the revolutionary potential of the urban working class as a result of the contradictions of the urban capitalist order. The Black Sea coast, with its manufacturing and shipping industries, was home to a large working class that the Marxist student factions in which Lev became involved viewed as an emerging revolutionary force in Russian society. Marxism was a theory fixated on the transformative power of capitalist networks of industry and manufacture, and the tendency of capitalism to engender social conflicts and contradictions that could only be resolved through a revolution that transferred the means of production to the workers themselves. Trotsky was in a place where such a perspective must have seemed very relevant, and he immediately began to act on his convictions.

Though always of an intellectual and theoretical disposition, Lev neglected his studies of mathematics and threw himself into writing for clandestine publications, circulating pamphlets, and organizing secret revolutionary organizations in Nikolayev and Odessa under the name of the South Russian Workers Union. This was exceedingly dangerous. In the wake of the assassination of Alexander II, the Russian police had begun to closely monitor all self-proclaimed radical groups and inflict harsh punishments on anyone they caught involved in anti-government organizations and activities.

When Lev and a number of his companions in the Workers Union were arrested in 1898, they had done little to put their ideas into action other than hold secret meetings and circulate pamphlets, but their incendiary publications and revolutionary intentions were enough to land them immediately in jail. Ironically, imprisonment seems to have had the effect of consolidating the convictions of many young Russian radicals, thus confirming their belief that revolution was the only way forward. Lev spent two years in jail in Odessa awaiting his sentence, and then found himself sentenced to exile and confinement in the same remote and harsh reaches of Siberia where Stalin would later build up an unparalleled network of prison camps. It was during his long imprisonment that he met and married his first wife, fellow radical Alexandra Sokolovskaya, with whom he had two children.

Alexandra, Lev (right), and Alexandra's brothers in 1897

It was also during this period that Lev widely read Marxist philosophy and theory, and he soon came into contact with those who would become his comrades in arms in revolution. Revolution would come sooner than most of them could anticipate.

Trotsky's writings even in 1901 displayed his dual senses of both revolution and optimism. In one 1901 work, he wrote:

> "If I were one of the celestial bodies, I would look with complete detachment upon this miserable ball of dust and dirt ... I would shine upon the good and the evil alike ... But I am a man. World history which to you, dispassionate gobbler of science, to you, book-keeper of eternity, seems only a negligible moment in the balance of time, is to me everything! As long as I breathe, I shall fight for the future, that radiant future in which man, strong and beautiful, will become master of the drifting stream of his history and will direct it towards the boundless horizon of beauty, joy, and happiness!
>
> The nineteenth century has in many ways satisfied and has in even more ways deceived the hopes of the optimist ... It has compelled him to transfer most of his hopes to twentieth century. Whenever the optimist was confronted by an atrocious fact, he exclaimed: What, and this can happen on the threshold of the twentieth century! When he drew wonderful pictured of the harmonious future, he placed them in the twentieth century.
>
> And now that century has come! What has it brought with it from the outset?
>
> In France – the poisonous foam of racial hatred; in Austria – nationalist strife ...; in South Africa – the agony of a tiny people, which is being murdered by a colossus; on the 'free' island itself – triumphant hymns to the victorious greed of jingoist jobbers; dramatic 'complications' in the east; rebellions of starving popular masses in Italy, Bulgaria, Romania ... Hatred and murder, famine and blood ..."

Chapter 4: Lenin Goes from Radical to Revolutionary

With his certification to practice law now firmly under his belt, Lenin returned to Samara and, in January of 1892, took a job as the legal assistant for a member of the regional court. For a man who was becoming gradually more committed to radically changing the nature of Russian government, it should come as no surprise that working for the government was not to his liking. As a result, he soon left to work for A.N. Khardin, a local lawyer whose practice was made up primarily of cases concerning peasants and other similarly needy people.

In spite of his new job, Lenin remained more interested in politics than the law and spent most of his evenings meeting with one or more of his fellow members in Skylarenko's political club. There they talked into the late hours of the night about the ideals of Karl Marx and how they could be applied to the problems facing the Russian people. Lenin became obsessed with collecting information and statistics about the Russian people that would support Marx's ideals about political and economic change.

Lenin gathered together his findings and presented them in a paper he submitted to the Russian Thought in 1893, but they refused to publish his work as it was written. While that work would not see the light of day again until a few years after his death, a few months later Lenin reproduced his research into a book called *On the So-Called Market Question*. In it he summed up his understanding of the plight of the peasants within the context of developing Russian capitalism:

"But only the prosperous peasant can enlarge his crop area, the one who has seed for sowing, and a sufficient quantity of livestock and implements. Such peasants (and they, as we know, are the minority) do, indeed, extend their crop areas and expand their farming to such an extent that they cannot cope with it without the aid of hired laborers. The majority of peasants, however, are quite unable to meet their need for money by expanding their farming, for they have no stocks, or sufficient means of production. Such a peasant, in order to obtain money, seeks "outside employments," i.e., takes his labor-power and not his product to the market. Naturally, work away from home entails a further decline in farming, and in the end the peasant leases his allotment to a rich fellow community member, who rounds off his farm and, of course, does not himself consume the product of the rented allotment, but sends it to the market. We get the "impoverishment of the people," the growth of capitalism and the expansion of the market. But that is not all. Our rich peasant, fully occupied by his extended farming, can no longer produce as hitherto for his own needs, let us say footwear: it is more advantageous for him to buy it. As to the impoverished peasant, he, too, has to buy footwear; he cannot produce it on his farm for the simple reason that he no longer has one. There arises a demand for footwear and a supply of grain, produced in abundance by the enterprising peasant, who touches the soul of Mr. V. V. with the progressive trend of his farming. The neighboring handicraft footwear-makers find themselves in the same position as the agriculturists just described: to buy grain, of which the declining farm yields too little, production must be expanded. Again, of course, production is expanded only by the handicraftsman who has savings, i.e., the representative of the minority; he is able to hire workers, or give work out to poor peasants to be done at home. The members of the majority of handicraftsmen, however, cannot even think of enlarging their workshops: they are glad to "get work" from the moneyed buyer-up, i.e., to find a purchaser of their only commodity—their labor-power. Again we get the impoverishment of the people, the growth of capitalism and the expansion of the market; a new impetus is given to the further development and intensification of the social division of labor."

Having arrived at his personal conclusions about what needed to be done Lenin returned to St.

Petersburg, where he got a job assisting lawyer M.F. Volenstein. There he joined S.I. Radchenko's radical group of "social democratic" students from the local Technical Institute, and, like in previous clubs, Lenin rapidly rose through the ranks. Inspired by the Marxist Social Democratic Party in Germany, they were thrilled to have the popular Lenin as a part of their group and chose him in January of 1894 to secretly debate author V.P. Vorontsov, known for his popular political tome *The Fate of Capitalism in Russia*. Unfortunately, the meeting was not entirely secret. A police officer was sent to monitor their talks and, when he reported what he had heard, the government realized that their old friend Lenin was at it again and stepped up their surveillance of his activities.

It was also around this time that Lenin had met Nadya Krupskaya, a schoolteacher who shared his Marxist leanings and eventually became his wife. She in turn introduced him to other members of her circle of socialist friends who regularly met on Sunday evenings to discuss politics, economics and other related topics. Though he was only in his 20s, Lenin's appearance surprised Nadya's friends, and they gave him the partially affectionate nickname of "old man." At the same time, though, they greatly respected his ideas and soon made him their discussion leader. With their help, he published "What the 'Friends of the People' Are and How They Fight the Social-Democrats," a political tract aimed at exposing those who opposed the political reforms of he and his friends. Now older and becoming ever more cautious, he published it under the pseudonym of Nikolai Petrovich, which he had adopted to avoid police attention.

Nadya

Lenin's writing brought him in conflict with more than just the police, however; he also had problems with the Socialist-Revolutionary Party over what role the peasantry should play in their plans for a new Russia. The SRP saw the peasants as a force to be reckoned with, since they outnumbered the proletariat by 75 to 1. On the other hand, Lenin and his fellow Marxists did not trust the farmers and small land owners, who they saw as simply being small-scale capitalists and part of the problem rather than the solution. In their minds, the future of the revolution lay in an uprising by the proletariat. At the time, the SRP's political inspiration was being provided by the writings of Marxist Georgi Plekhanov, who wrote under the pseudonym "Narodnaya Volga," the last name of the nom de guerre provided by Russia's famous river. It is assumed that when Vladimir used the nom de guerre Lenin for the first time in December 1901, it was a reference to the River Lena and thus an imitation of Plekhanov's pseudonym.

Plekhanov

Hoping to solidify relations between the Russian socialists and those of the rest of Europe, Lenin spent the next several years travelling to several other countries promoting his ideas. Perhaps hoping that being away from Russia would keep him out of jail, Maria financed much of his travel. Lenin first went to Switzerland where, in 1895, he met with several members of the Liberation Labor party. While in Geneva, he was able to meet with the organizer of the Emancipation of Labor Party, who encouraged Lenin to reconsider his perspective on the role of the bourgeoisie in his future plans. From there he went to Zurich, then Paris, where he met with members of the Paris Commune of 1871, before returning to Switzerland and resting in a popular health spa. Then he went on to Berlin, where he spent six weeks studying and meeting with socialist leaders.

Lenin returned to Russia in 1895, his head filled with new ideas and his bags with illegal books and pamphlets. When the workers at St. Petersburg's Thornton textile mill went on strike, Lenin and his followers were there passing out tracts and urging them on. This, along with his latest publication, "The Worker's Cause", proved to be the final straw for the Russian government. Lenin was arrested along with 40 of his fellow activists.

Lenin's 1895 police mugshot

Lenin denied that he had done anything wrong, but was imprisoned in the House of Preliminary Detention while the government put together its case against him. Though Maria and his siblings attempted to intervene on his behalf, he was not granted bail and thus remained in jail during the year leading up to his trial. Lenin was, however, allowed paper and pens, which allowed him to spend most of his time writing on his new favorite topic, class consciousness. By the time he was sentenced, he had completed "Draft and Explanation of a Programme for the Social Democratic Party" and had started writing "The Development of Capitalism in Russia", an attack on the platform of the SRP that he would finish in exile .

In February, 1897, Lenin and his fellow political prisoners were sentenced, without trial, to three years in Siberia. In a surprising show of compassion, the government allowed him a few days of freedom before his departure. Lenin spent this time catching up on the changes that had happened in the Social-Democratic Party during his absence. The most significant of these was that it was now known as the League of Struggle for the Emancipation of the Working Class. Also, with so many of its leader in prison, the common workers had risen to positions of authority, to Lenin's dubious satisfaction.

When he left St. Petersburg for the treacherous 11 hour trip to Shushenskyoye, his mind was no doubt full of politics and plans for the future. However, he likely also regretted leaving behind Nadya Krupskaya, with whom he was romantically involved. However, their parting would not be forever; instead, she joined him in his exile in 1898 after being sentenced to Siberia herself for helping to organize a strike in August of 1896. Ironically, the two atheists were married to each other in a church on July 10, 1898.

As he had in the past, Lenin spent his time in exile reading, studying and writing. He published The Tasks of Russian Social Democrats, in which he concluded:

"Russian Social-Democracy is still faced with an enormous, almost untouched field of work. The awakening of the Russian working class, its spontaneous striving for knowledge, organisation, socialism, for the struggle against its exploiters and oppressors becomes more widespread, more strikingly apparent every day. The enormous progress made by Russian capitalism in recent times is a guarantee that the working-class movement will grow uninterruptedly in breadth and depth. We are apparently now passing through the period in the capitalist cycle when industry is "prospering," when business is brisk, when the factories are working at full capacity and when countless new factories, new enterprises, joint-stock companies, railway enterprises, etc., etc., are springing up like mushrooms. One need not be a prophet to foretell the inevitable and fairly sharp crash that is bound to succeed this period of industrial "prosperity." This crash will ruin masses of small owners, will throw masses of workers into the ranks of the unemployed, and will thus confront all the workers in an acute form with the problems of socialism and democracy which have long faced every class-conscious, every thinking worker. Russian Social-Democrats must see to it that when this crash comes the Russian proletariat is more class-conscious, more united, able to understand the tasks of the Russian working class, capable of putting up resistance to the capitalist class—which is now reaping huge profits and always strives to burden the workers with the losses—and capable of leading Russian democracy in a decisive struggle against the police autocracy, which binds and fetters the Russian workers and the whole of the Russian people."

In addition, Lenin wrote pamphlets and shorter pieces for socialist journals. Then, with Nadya's help, he also translated *The Theory and Practice of Trade Unionism* by Sidney and Beatrice Webb from English into Russian.

When Lenin was released in 1900 he had to leave Nadya behind to finish serving her sentence. He traveled with his new colleague, Jewish socialist Jules Martov, to Geneva. There they met with one of their heroes, Georgi Plekhanov, the author of *The Development of the Monist View of History*. Operating under his well known pseudonym, Plekhanov was considered to be one of the founders of Russian Marxism, and he had fled Russia for Switzerland after his writings became too unpopular. However, much to Lenin's disappointment, Plekhanov proved very difficult to work with. The older man was suspicious of Lenin, seeing him as a young upstart who wanted to take control of his life's work. He was also very anti-Semitic, and soon offended Martov with his outspoken and rude remarks. Of course, Plekhanov was hardly the only anti-Semitic Russian, which was a source of consternation to Lenin throughout his life. Lenin would later write, "It is not the Jews who are the enemies of the working people. The enemies of the workers are the capitalists of all countries. Among the Jews there are working people, and they form the majority. They are our brothers, who, like us, are oppressed by capital; they are our comrades in the struggle for socialism…Shame on those who foment hatred towards the Jews…"

Copy of the first edition of Iskra

Though the men remained members of the Liberation of Labor, they decided to begin publishing that new paper, Iskra, in Germany so that Plekhanov could not get his hands on it. Iskra would soon become the official paper of the Social Democratic Labour Party, formed with the intent gather the scattered social revolutionary groups under its one umbrella organization in the hopes of overthrowing the Russian government. Operating for more than 50 years, many of them illegally and underground, Iskra would prove to be one of Lenin's crowning achievements. While he had to secretly smuggle copies into Russia, he was still able to attract some of the finest minds in European socialism to write for the paper. Among these were Rosa Luxemburg from Poland and one of Lenin's fellow Russians.

Luxemburg

Chapter 5: The Birth of Leon Trotsky

While Trotsky was in prison in Odessa, the Russian Social Democratic Labor Party was founded. While he was obviously blocked from direct participation in the formation of the party, he was able to get word of its first congress and follow its developments from afar. It was the moment Russian Marxists had been waiting for: the founding of a major movement that represented and pursued their agenda.

Obviously, the Tsarist police worked hard to strangle the infant movement in its cradle. The leaders who were not quickly arrested and exiled were wise enough to go into exile themselves. Many of the party members formed a core group in London and began publishing the newspaper *Iskra* ("Spark"), whose editorial board included the young Vladimir Ulyanov (Lenin) and the elder statesman of Russian Marxism, Georgi Plekhanov, who had been personally acquainted with Friedrich Engels himself. Plekhanov had been in exile for decades, while Ulyanov (Lenin) and Julius Martov, another influential editor, were of about the same generation as Trotsky and had only recently fled police persecution in Russia.

Lenin

Plekhanov

It was only two years into his Siberian exile that Lev Davidovich Bronshtein successfully fled the country with forged papers identifying him as Leon Trotsky, which at that point became his primary surname for the rest of his life. He left behind his young wife and their two baby daughters, with whom he would never live again. He and Alexandra divorced, and their children were raised partly by the Bronshteins in the Ukraine after leaving Siberia. In essence, Trotsky made a decisive break with his life at the exact same moment that took on an adopted name. By the time he returned to Russia, nothing would be the same, least of all his own position there. He left in 1902 as an obscure exiled radical, but he would return as a leader at the vanguard of a surging revolutionary movement, with Tsarism apparently breathing its last breaths.

Not surprisingly, Trotsky's destination was London, where he was quickly absorbed into the circle around *Iskra*. Trotsky began by publishing numerous articles under the *nom de plume* Pero. Although he may have imagined he would find a united front of like-minded revolutionaries, he soon found that the London community of radical Russian exiles was actually fractured along generational and ideological lines. In fact, the rifts that would turn the early Soviet Union into a bloody theater of factionalism were already taking shape. Lenin and Martov, who saw in the young newcomer a like-minded man of similar age and experiences, were eager to enlist his support for their more action-oriented group. In March 1903, Lenin wrote:

> "I suggest to all the members of the editorial board that they co-opt 'Pero' as a member of the board on the same basis as other members. [...] We very much need a seventh member, both as a convenience in voting (six being an even number), and as an addition to our forces. 'Pero' has been contributing to every issue for several months now; he works in general most energetically for the Iskra; he gives lectures (in which he has been very successful). In the section of articles and notes on the events of the day, he will not only be very useful, but absolutely necessary. Unquestionably a man of rare abilities, he has conviction and energy, and he will go much farther."

However, when Lenin and Martov attempted to make Trotsky part of the editorial board of *Iskra*, the move was blocked by Plekhanov.

In order to understand the conflicts that divided the Russian exile community, it is important to consider the difficulty of applying Marxist revolutionary theory to the Russian context. Marx and Engels had written the *Communist Manifesto* in the years leading up to the European Revolutions of 1848, a series of revolts that shook the countries of Western Europe with a great deal of involvement from the growing industrial working class. For Marx, communist revolution was a necessary consequence of the contradictions created by industrialization and the rise of the middle class or bourgeoisie, which itself had overthrown the rule of the *ancien régime* and installed electoral democratic government by male property owners in varying degrees across Western Europe. Marx and Engels argued that the industrial working class, whose labor fueled the growing wealth of the bourgeoisie, did not benefit from the bourgeois freedoms achieved by the French Revolution and like-minded liberal reforms. To them, the working class' "freedom" was merely a freedom to sell their labor, which indentured them to the propertied classes. As industrialization and commerce spread, Marx and Engels argued, the class of dispossessed workers would grow and eventually demand its own liberation in the form of control of the means of production or machinery of industry.

While these prescriptions were understood to ultimately apply to the world as a whole, the obvious hotbeds of revolution in Marxist theory should have been northern England and the Rhine Valley of northwestern Germany, the most industrialized and proletarianized regions of Europe. But things did not unfold that way. Influential socialist parties did emerge in those places, but for the most part they found success by demanding reform through the "bourgeois" political system. While Marx and Engels took it for granted that the bourgeois would not give up control or power, instead of becoming more repressive and reactionary in response to the burgeoning demands for workers' rights, the bourgeois in the Rhine Valley and northern England saw fit to accommodate some of the demands of the working class. By being more compromising, they reduced the potential for the kind of revolutionary explosion predicted by Marx and Engels.

At the time that Trotsky and his fellow Russians were plotting revolution in London, the evidence that history had not followed Marx's prophesies to the letter was clear enough to see, but the question of exactly how Marxists should respond to these developments was a major source of strife. This was especially true when it came to the vexing problem of revolution in a largely rural country like Russia, which had not even undergone a bourgeois liberal revolution yet.

In light of the Marxist perspectives just discussed, there were two major questions those who sought revolution in Russia had to confront. First, how quickly could Russia undergo a full-scale communist revolution when it had not yet thoroughly undergone the processes of industrialization, urbanization, and liberal reform that Marx had viewed as essential precursors to the proletarian revolution? There were pockets of advanced industrial development in Russia, including places along the Black Sea coast where Trotsky had cut his political teeth, but for the most part it was a traditional rural country that far more resembled the pre-revolutionary French *ancien régime* than the modern industrial cities Marx had seen as ripe for communist revolt. Did Russia first need to undergo a bourgeois liberal revolution and a period of industrialization before Marxism could even become a viable political philosophy there?

Plekhanov was already in disagreement with Lenin and Martov on this issue by the time Trotsky arrived in London. Plekhanov was more orthodox in the sense that he believed a bourgeois revolution and a period of liberal rule, commercial liberalization, and industrialization were necessary precursors to any movement toward communism. In this account of things, the role of Marxists should be to allow liberal reformers to move history forward in a progressive direction and to help organize the growing working class. Naturally, the younger generation was less content to sit on their hands; Lenin and Martov thought Plekhanov's gradualist approach was out of touch with the realities of contemporary Russia, where they had seen the seeds of radical revolt everywhere. On top of that, they knew as well as anyone that the Tsarist regime was more reactionary and entrenched than ever.

However, while Lenin and Martov shared an impatience for the doctrinaire Marxist approaches of their elders, the two were divided over how to make their revolution happen. Should Russian Marxists attempt to bring about change by democratic means in broad coalition with other progressive groups, or should they make use of violent and secretive methods closer to those of the Narodniks and other Russian populist and anarchist groups? It was on this question, particularly acute in a period in which many European socialist parties were operating successfully within democratic systems, that the fateful Bolshevik and Menshevik factions were initially created. The Mensheviks, who followed Martov's thinking, proposed a broad-based, inclusive party open to democratic processes but generally representative of workers' interests and causes.

Martov

Lenin's Bolsheviks, in contrast, emphasized a small and strictly disciplined party organization that was tightly controlled by professional revolutionaries who could lead and orchestrate all action. Trotsky was critical of Lenin's path, and he prophetically wrote at the time, "Lenin's methods lead to this: the party organization substitutes itself for the party, the central committee substitutes itself for the organization, and, finally, a 'dictator' substitutes himself for the central committee. ... The party must seek the guarantee of its stability in its own base, in an active and self-reliant proletariat, and not in its top caucus ... which the revolution may suddenly sweep away with its wing."

The conflicts came to a head at the congress of the Social Democratic Labor Party in London in 1903, with Trotsky originally siding with Martov and the Mensheviks but later declaring himself independent of the key factions. But the more Trotsky attempted to bridge the differences between the rivals, the more he found himself subject to mistrust from members of both groups. While he would ultimately and decisively throw his lot in with Lenin, Trotsky's failure to become a Bolshevik in this early period would much later be seized upon by his political enemies as evidence of his disloyalty and his unauthentic commitment to Lenin's agenda within the Soviet Union.

It was at about this time that the former Ulyanov took the name Lenin as his official nom de guerre. Nadya was also released from Siberia and joined her husband in Munich, where she worked as his personal secretary and helped produce Iskra. In 1903 he wrote To the Village Poor, in which he conceded the Social Revolutionary Party's point about the importance of the peasant population to the political future of Russia. Thus in this pamphlet he appealed to them to rise up against the Russian aristocracy and join the socialist cause.

Rosa Luxemburg, one of the early writers for Iskra, soon spotted a flaw in Lenin's plan. She criticized his plan for a centralized government that would place all the power of lawmaking in the hands of a few intellectually superior leaders. She concluded:

> "In general, it is rigorous, despotic centralism that is preferred by opportunist intellectuals at a time when the revolutionary elements among the workers still lack cohesion and the movement is groping its way, as is the case now in Russia. In a later phase, under a parliamentary regime and in connection with a strong labor party, the opportunist tendencies of the intellectuals express themselves in an inclination toward "decentralization." If we assume the viewpoint claimed as his own by Lenin and we fear the influence of intellectuals in the proletarian movement, we can conceive of no greater danger to the Russian party than Lenin's plan of organization. Nothing will more surely enslave a young labor movement to an intellectual elite hungry for power than this bureaucratic straightjacket, which will immobilize the movement and turn it into an automaton manipulated by a Central Committee. On the other hand there is no more effective guarantee against opportunist intrigue and personal ambition than the independent revolutionary action of the proletariat, as a result of which the workers acquire the sense of political responsibility and self-reliance. What is today only a phantom haunting Lenin's imagination may become reality tomorrow."

Meanwhile, in *The Proletariat and the Revolution* (1904), Trotsky wrote about the importance of revolutionary action, even if it doesn't take a visibly militant form:

> "The proletariat must not only conduct a revolutionary propaganda. The proletariat itself must move towards a revolution.
>
> To move towards a revolution does not necessarily mean to fix a date for an insurrection and to prepare for that day. You never can fix a day and an hour for a revolution. The people have never made a revolution by command.
>
> What can be done is, in view of the fatally impending catastrophe, to choose the most appropriate positions, to arm and inspire the masses with a revolutionary slogan, to lead simultaneously all the reserves into the field of battle, to make them practice in the art of fighting, to keep them ready under arms, – and to send an alarm all over the lines when the time has arrived.

Would that mean a series of exercises only, and not a decisive combat with the enemy forces? Would that be mere manoeuvers, and not a street revolution?

Yes, that would be mere manoeuvers. There is a difference, however, between revolutionary and military manoeuvers. Our preparations can turn, at any time and independent of our will, into a real battle which would decide the long drawn revolutionary war. Not only can it be so, it must be. This is vouched for by the acuteness of the present political situation which holds in its depths a tremendous amount of revolutionary explosives.

At what time mere manoeuvers would turn into a real battle, depends upon the volume and the revolutionary compactness of the masses, upon the atmosphere of popular sympathy which surrounds them and upon the attitude of the troops which the government moves against the people."

At the same time, Trotsky began to dedicate himself as early as 1904 to elaborating what would become his major contribution to Marxist thought: the theory of permanent revolution. The theory of permanent revolution was an attempt to account for how socialism could be achieved in a so-called "backwards" country like Russia, which had not reached the level of capitalist development presented by Marx as necessary for the emergence of a proletarian revolutionary movement. He wrote, "It is our interest and our task to make the revolution permanent until all the more or less propertied classes have been driven from their ruling positions, until the proletariat has conquered state power and until the association of the proletarians has progressed sufficiently far – not only in one country but in all the leading countries of the world – that competition between the proletarians of these countries ceases and at least the decisive forces of production are concentrated in the hands of the workers. ... Their battle-cry must be: 'The Permanent Revolution'."

While Trotsky certainly sided with Lenin and Martov on the need for immediate action, his initial refusal to throw in his lot with either the Bolsheviks or the Mensheviks was in part determined by his sense that neither group had developed a sound theoretical account of how revolution would in fact come about in Russia. Neither had developed an alternative to the notion that Russia would need to undergo a bourgeois liberal revolution, followed by a period of democratic rule and industrialization, before it could move toward the stage of communist revolution. Permanent revolution was supposed to be an alternative to this "two-stage" theory of political development.

Trotsky, initially in collaboration with fellow Russian exile Alexander Parvus, developed permanent revolution out of some scattered remarks by Marx and Engels that make use of this phrase to refer to the permanently oppositional status of proletarian movements. The key claim of Trotsky's and Parvus's theory was that the Russian bourgeoisie itself was too perennially weak and ineffectual to move the country politically toward the kind of liberal reforms achieved in Western Europe a century earlier. Industrialization in Russia had proceeded to generate a large proletariat through much of the country in advance of any recognizable political liberalization. Given the weakness of the Russian bourgeoisie and the retrenched power of the reactionary Tsarist state, it would fall to the proletariat, in collaboration with the dispossessed rural peasantry, to spearhead any and all political reform. But since the means of production would need to undergo a prolonged development in order to achieve the degree of productivity necessary for an advanced industrial economy, the revolutionary classes would have to oversee a period of "permanent revolution", in which the country would progress toward the adequate conditions for the genuine development of socialism. At the same time, the revolution would have to permanently expand outward in order to foster alliances internationally that would counterbalance the inevitable resurgence of reactionary enemies.

There were significant developments in Trotsky's personal life during his London years as well. After his divorce from Alexandra, who was still in Russia, he met fellow exile Natalia Sedova and married her shortly afterward. Interestingly, Trotsky took her last name, noting, "In order not to oblige my sons to change their name, I, for 'citizenship' requirements, took on the name of my wife." Trotsky and Sedova would have two sons, but like his two daughters from his first marriage, they would die before him.

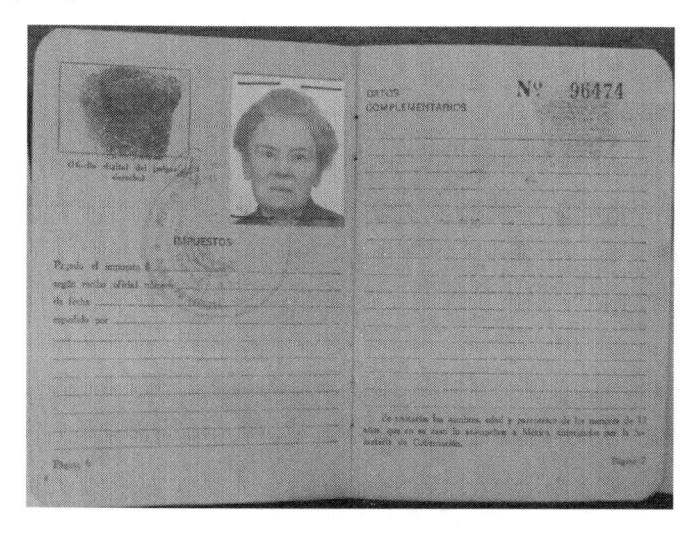

Natalia's passport

Despite the twists and turns of Trotsky's later life, Natalia would remain his companion until the end. Once again, though, Trotsky was only about two years into marriage when his domestic life was dramatically disrupted, this time by a surprising chain of events back in Russia. Quite suddenly, the discussions of revolution by the young men in London would cease to be mere theoretical debates

Chapter 6: Stalin Gets Involved

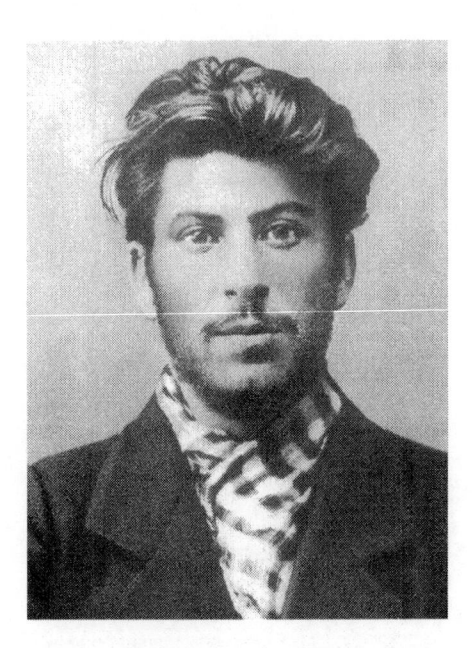

Stalin in the early 1900s

With an incomplete education, Stalin had problems getting work. On the one hand, professional fields were not an option because he had no degree. On the other hand, he felt menial labor was beneath his dignity. Finally, he got a job tutoring children and, later, working as a clerk. These, however, were simply to allow him to eat. His true vocation lay in writing. He soon became a regular contributor to Brdzola Khma Vladimir, a socialist newspaper based out of Georgia.

Stalin made his first serious foray into politics in 1901, when he joined the Social Democratic Labor Party, whose main goal was to overthrow the Tsar through industrial organization and resistance. His activities within the party led to his first arrest in April of 1902, when he was sentenced to 18 months in prison for organizing a strike among the workers of a large factory in Batum, Georgia. Even after his stay in prison, however, his captors were still concerned that he was going to continue to be a problem, so they exiled him to the famed Russian frozen dessert,

Siberia.

Not surprisingly, the determined Stalin didn't stay in Siberia long. Shortly after that Congress, Stalin escaped in 1904 and quickly made his way back to Tiflis, where he once again began inciting workers to strike. Upon learning that the Social Democrats had split into two rival factions, Stalin naturally chose the Bolsheviks due to his admiration of Lenin. These activities brought him to the attention of his hero, Vladimir Lenin, who invited him to Tampere, Finland in late 1905 for a conference of Bolshevik leaders. Stalin was duly impressed by the massive gathering of workers and revolutionaries. He was also intrigued by the concept of democratic centralism, a mode of government that Lenin described as "freedom of discussion, unity of action."

Completely committed to Lenin's teachings, Stalin spent the next eight years of his life promoting democratic centralism throughout Russia. Though his efforts got him arrested on four more occasions, he was never held long before escaping. One has to wonder at the ease with which he was able to thwart the efforts of such a supposedly harsh system. Perhaps his jailors were sympathetic to his cause or, more likely, their sympathy was bought by bribes from his fellow political rebels.

It was also in the middle of the decade that Stalin met and married his first wife, Ekaterina "Kato" Svanidze, and they had their first child, a son, in 1907. When she died later that same year of typhus, Stalin lamented at her funeral, "This creature softened my heart of stone. She died and with her died my last warm feelings for humanity." His feelings for her would not stop him from killing several members of his first wife's family during the Great Purge, including her sister Mariko and brother Alexander.

Ekaterina

Chapter 7: Revolutionary Activities Abroad

"How invincibly eloquent are facts! How utterly powerless are words! The masses have made themselves heard! They have kindled revolutionary flames on Caucasian hill-tops; they have clashed, breast against breast, with the guards' regiments and the Cossacks on that unforgettable day of January Ninth; they have filled the streets and squares of industrial cities with the noise and clatter of their fights ..." – Leon Trotsky, 1905

By the beginning of 1905, Russia was a veritable pressure cooker, exploding with political and social tensions in all sectors of society. In the major cities, industrial production had grown at a dizzying pace under the policies of Sergei Witte, Tsar Nicholas II's finance minister, creating a large dislocated urban underclass of precisely the sort that Marx had seen as the vanguard of revolution. The countryside was also teeming with discontent; when the serfs had been released from bondage, they had been given loans that were to finance the purchase of small holdings, a program that the tsarist government hoped would turn them into a large class of conservative property holders. But the generally small incomes Russian peasants were able to earn had left them crushed by mortgage payments they were often unable to make in full, and with little hope that they would be able to get out from under the debt they had incurred. Finally, the disastrous Russo-Japanese war left Russia broke and humiliated, creating widespread discontent among the populace.

In general, the government responded to expressions of protest with the kind of heavy-handed tactics that were applied to the young activists during the previous decade. This left very few confident that their grievances could be resolved through peaceful negotiation. The appeal of more radical approaches increased.

The Russian Revolution of 1905 began in a way that firebrands like Trotsky would have regarded as inauspicious. On Sunday, January 22, there was a peaceful march led by a Russian Orthodox priest, in which the protesters were carrying signs reading "Long Live the Tsar!" Inspired by the strikes that had overtaken a number of factories around St. Petersburg, the protesters intended to deliver to the Tsar himself a respectful petition of moderate demands for reform and dialogue. But upon arriving at the Winter Palace, the group was instructed by guards to turn back, and when it failed to do so, the guards began to fire indiscriminately into the crowd. A chaotic stampede followed, increasing the casualties.

Estimates of the number of deaths vary, but even the surely too conservative estimate of the Tsar's own regime counted 200 casualties, and most independently issued numbers are much higher. The massacre followed the pattern the revolutionaries knew all too well, where even peaceful voicing of dissent encountered a response so harsh that it allows for no dialogue, thus exacerbating the discontent into outright revolt. Such a radicalization is precisely what happened, on a countrywide scale, in the final week of January 1905.

The news of "Bloody Sunday" spread like wildfire across the Russian Empire, prompting massive strikes in its major cities, but the regime did not learn from its first mistake. More protesters were massacred in Riga and Warsaw within days of the initial slaughter in St. Petersburg. The strikes ultimately spread from factory workers to students and railway workers, leading to the forced paralysis of universities and railway lines. Ultimately and crucially, a series of mutinies began in the military, culminating in the famous mutiny of the *Battleship Potemkin* in Trotsky's former home city of Odessa, later immortalized in Eisenstein's eponymous film.

Meanwhile, some of the remotest parts of the Empire were highly susceptible to the unrest, as local ethnic populations such as the Georgians, Armenians, Poles, Finns, and Baltic peoples had been seething for decades about the "Russification" policies that forced them to subordinate themselves culturally to Russia. Their demands for cultural autonomy and national self-determination mixed with the clamor for workers' rights and the economic grievances of the rural peasantry to create a state of fragmentation and chaos. When the Tsar's uncle, Grand Duke Sergei Alexandrovich, was assassinated by a bomb placed in his carriage, the Tsar finally decided to accept negotiation over reform. By late February, he accepted the principle of a broadened right to assembly and right of free speech, as well as reform measures to lessen the debt of the peasants and some form of popular political representation.

The Tsar's negotiations, mainly with elite liberal reformists, continued throughout the year as the country continued to explode with unrest among nearly every social group. In October of 1905, the Tsar reluctantly agreed to put his signature on a document that significantly expanded citizens' rights and created a clear path towards democratic governance, including universal suffrage. Although strikes and protests continued and were often met with brutal responses from the army and police, the October Manifesto, as it was called, gained widespread support because it seemed to leave the door open to further change by democratic means. There was also a large-scale amnesty of prisoners, which seemed to placate some of the popular rage.

However, the Russian people were exhausted by the end of 1905. The protests had led to thousands or even tens of thousands of deaths over the preceding year, as well as massive destruction of property and disruption of life. The populace had shown itself capable of bringing the entire country to a dead halt through synchronized strikes, but the Tsar's surprising willingness to compromise and open the door to reform had quelled tensions to some degree for the moment.

Naturally, the men in London were overjoyed by the events in 1905, especially because they viewed it as a fulfillment of their prophecy. Trotsky wrote:

> "The revolutionary masses are no more a theory, they are a fact. For the Social-Democratic Party there is nothing new in this fact. We had predicted it long ago. We had seen its coming at a time when the noisy liberal banquets seemed to form a

striking contrast with the political silence of the people. The revolutionary masses are a fact, was our assertion. The clever liberals shrugged their shoulders in contempt. Those gentlemen think themselves sober realists solely because they are unable to grasp the consequences of great causes, because they make it their business to be humble servants of each ephemeral political fact. They think themselves sober statesmen in spite of the fact that history mocks at their wisdom, tearing to pieces their schoolbooks, making to naught their designs, and magnificently laughing at their pompous predictions.

'There are no revolutionary people in Russia as yet' 'The Russian workingman is backward in culture, in self-respect, and (we refer primarily to the workingmen of Petersburg and Moscow) he is not yet prepared for organized social and political struggle.'…

Yes, the Revolution has begun. We had hoped for it, we had had no doubt about it. For long years, however, it had been to us a mere deduction from our "doctrine," which all nonentities of all political denominations had mocked at. They never believed in the revolutionary role of the proletariat, yet they believed in the power of Zemstvo petitions, in Witte, in "blocs" combining naughts with naughts, in Svyatopolk-Mirski, in a stick of dynamite … There was no political superstition they did not believe in. Only the belief in the proletariat to them was a superstition,

History, however, does not question political oracles, and the revolutionary people do not need a passport from political eunuchs."

In a similar vein, Lenin wrote, "Only the most ignorant people can close their eyes to the bourgeois nature of the democratic revolution which is now taking place. Whoever wants to reach socialism by any other path than that of political democracy will inevitably arrive at conclusions that are absurd and reactionary both in the economic and the political sense."

Trotsky's role in the 1905 Revolution was both marginal and crucial. By the time Trotsky arrived in the country after the long journey from London, the strikes were already well underway, and many important political developments had occurred before he could make any impact on the trajectory of the revolution. He and the socialist leadership in London had had relatively little role in inciting any of the revolts; pus simply, a number of sectors of the population without a particularly confrontational political agenda had been radicalized by the events of Bloody Sunday and similar acts of unprovoked brutality on the part of the Tsarist government. That's not to say the 1905 Revolution ran counter to the basic Marxist theory of class struggle, since Marx and Engels believed the masses would be spontaneously led to revolt by the sheer exploitation and oppression to which they were being subjected. Whatever its general applicability, this was a fairly good description of what occurred in the Russian Empire in 1905. But the principal role of intellectuals like Trotsky in such a context, at least initially, was largely to catch up with events and determine the most advantageous role to be played in them. This is what he and his Menshevik and Bolshevik comrades tried to do.

Trotsky's role may also be regarded as crucial, however, because he continued to do his best to bridge the divide between Bolshevik and Menshevik, and in so doing, he became a leader with general appeal among the industrial workers then in revolt. While the theoretical differences between the two camps may have seemed all-consuming in their clandestine meetings in exile, in the heat of the struggles of 1905 they probably would have seemed petty and irrelevant to most of those actually involved in the strike. In the process of pursuing his "big tent" approach, Trotsky became one of the key figures in the St. Petersburg Soviet, which in turn made him an important part of what was probably the most important institutional development for the Russian workers movement during the revolutionary period. "Soviet" is a Russian word translatable to "council," but the St. Petersburg Soviet was the first open council of workers to gather and organize for workers' interests. It was created with some Menshevik involvement prior to Trotsky's appearance, but by dint of his charisma and rhetoric of unity he quickly rose to the position of vice chairman and then chairman by the end of 1905. When the Soviet was created, there had been no previous widely attended assembly intended to support the interests of the urban industrial workers, separate from the labor unions, which were regarded as highly compromised through government infiltration. Thus, from the perspective of radicals like Trotsky, the creation of the Soviet was a vital part of the process of making the proletarian revolution a reality.

In the meantime, the Russian imperial government and its elite liberal partners in dialogue were eager to do away with the more radical elements of the revolutionary sectors of society. For Trotsky and the other representatives of the Soviet, negotiation with the Tsar and piecemeal reform would have been nothing more than a ploy to squash the unstoppable momentum of the revolutionary movement that had been building throughout the year. Thus, to the radical revolutionaries, the October Manifesto was simply a reactionary sham that changed nothing about the basic necessity of revolt and resistance.

While the Tsarist government had loosened some of its restrictions on public speech critical of the Tsar and had opened the way to reforms that would have been unimaginable just a year earlier, after the October Manifesto the regime decided to clamp down on its more radical critics. The St. Petersburg Soviet was shuttered, and its leaders, including Trotsky, were arrested in late 1905 after refusing to recognize the authority of the government and announcing a new general strike to stop the piecemeal reforms. A new wave of repression, radiating out across the country, accompanied these arrests.

As the liberal reformist class negotiated with its new conservative interlocutors about the creation of a parliamentary monarchy, long-exiled Marxists like Trotsky found themselves in the same position they had been in at the turn of the century. They went from being political prisoners to being exiled. But if Trotsky had impressed the assembled workers of the Soviet with his speaking abilities, his blistering speech to the Tsarist court that brought him to trial in 1906 further consolidated his growing reputation for eloquence. He concluded his remarks to the court as follows:

> "The prosecution invites us to admit that the Soviet armed the workers for the struggle against the existing 'form of government.' If I am categorically asked whether this was so, I shall answer: Yes! Yes, I am willing to accept this accusation. [But] let me ask: what does the prosecution mean by 'form of government'? Do we really have a form of government? For a long time past the government has not been supported by the nation but only by its military-police apparatus. What we have is not a national government but an automaton for mass murder. I can find no other name for the government machine which is tearing into parts the living body of our country. If you tell me that the pogroms, the murders, the burnings, the rapes . . . are the form of government of the Russian Empire – then I will agree with the prosecution that in October and November last we were arming ourselves, directly and immediately, against the form of government of the Russian Empire."

In retrospect, it is tempting to regard Trotsky as a prophet. Ultimately, the constitutional and parliamentary monarchy that was emerging out of the negotiations between Tsarists and liberals would fail, in large part because it was perceived by many as mere window dressing for the continued reactionary and repressive rule that preceded it and the brutal military apparatus that propped it up. But at the time, Trotsky's return to Siberian exile may have looked like a disastrous failure for what had been a workers' movement with unstoppable momentum. The 1905 Revolution certainly failed to bring about the desired effect that Lenin and other revolutionaries hoped it would, leading Lenin to believe that more forceful revolting was a necessity. A few years after the 1905 Revolution, Lenin would write:

> "Notwithstanding all the differences in the aims and tasks of the Russian revolution, compared with the French revolution of 1871, the Russian proletariat had to resort to the same method of struggle as that first used by the Paris Commune — civil war. Mindful of the lessons of the Commune, it knew that the proletariat should not ignore peaceful methods of struggle — they serve its ordinary, day-to-day interests, they are necessary in periods of preparation for revolution — but it must never forget that in certain conditions the class struggle assumes the form of armed conflict and civil war; there are times when the interests of the proletariat call for ruthless extermination of its enemies in open armed clashes."

Though Lenin was back in Russia during these events, he showed little interest in the changes.

Instead, he chose to bide his time and wait for the people to again despair of real hope within the current regime. In fact, he even encouraged his fellow Bolsheviks to take part in the Duma Elections of 1907, while he devoted his own time to raising money for future political activity.

It quickly becomes obvious that Lenin's fundraising methods went far beyond the modern concept of the thousand dollar a plate rubber chicken dinner. In addition to soliciting large donations from self-made Russian millionaires like Sava Morozov and Maxim Gorky, he also relied very heavily on donations raised through bank robberies successfully planned and executed by Bolshevik gangs. One such robbery, in which several people were killed, drew the ire of the Mensheviks, who began to distance themselves even further from Lenin and his followers.

It may have seemed at odds with Lenin's declaration at the Second Congress that violence and terror would not be accepted, but Lenin apparently had no scruples regarding how to finance his activities. Lenin converted most of the money into documents and utilized various papers and pamphlets he printed in an attempt to raise the political awareness of the general population of Russia. When that failed, he bribed leaders of the trade unions to influence their members toward socialism. He even went so far as to get one of his favorite men, Roman Malinovsky, elected to the head of the Metalworker's Union in St. Petersburg. This would prove to be a huge mistake.

Malinovsky

Forced by increasing scandal and suspicion to once again leave Russia, Lenin spent the next several months in seclusion. It was during this time that he created his most significant work, *Materialism and Empirio-criticism*. Published in secret in 1909, this book outlined the foundations for what is now referred to as Marxism-Leninism. In it he quotes everyone from philosophers and bishops to politicians and physicists in an attempt to prove that materialism is the root of all political evil. Writing at length about reason and nature, Lenin expounds upon philosophy, with quotes like, "The sole 'property' of matter with whose recognition philosophical materialism is bound up is the property of being an objective reality, of existing outside the mind."

Lenin left Russia again in 1911, this time moving to France to found the Bolshevik Party School to train political activists outside the prying eyes of the Russian police. He also devoted much of his time to meetings with his associates on how the Bolsheviks could take control of the Social Democratic Labor Party. However, when the 1912 annual meeting was held in Prague, he was unable to rally the votes in his favor. Instead, the Bolsheviks and Mensheviks split from each other completely and, from that day forward, maintained completely separate organizations. Such splinters didn't deter Lenin, who wholeheartedly supported removing those not fully committed to the same cause from the group. Around the time of the Second Congress, it was Lenin who noted, "Everyone is free to write and say whatever he likes, without any restrictions. But every voluntary association (including the party) is also free to expel members who use the name of the party to advocate anti-party views. Freedom of speech and the press must be complete. But then freedom of association must be complete too. I am bound to accord you, in the name of free speech, the full right to shout, lie and write to your heart's content. But you are bound to grant me, in the name of freedom of association, the right to enter into, or withdraw from, association with people advocating this or that view. The party is a voluntary association, which would inevitably break up, first ideologically and then physically, if it did not cleanse itself of people advocating anti-party views."

Though the revolutionary cause now had two disparate factions, Lenin did have one major success in Prague. He convinced the members to elect Malinovsky to the Bolshevik Central Committee, in spite of rumors that he was in fact a spy for the Okhrana, the Russian secret police. Lenin also convinced the party to run Malinovsky as a candidate for the Duma. They did, and he was elected in 1912, bringing the number of Bolsheviks in the Duma to six. Malinovsky soon distinguished himself among the group for his leadership and speaking abilities. Before giving any speech, however, he would send a copy to Lenin for his comments. What Lenin didn't know was that he was also sending a copy to the head of the Okhrana.

Armed with previews of speeches being made, as well as copies of letters exchanged between Lenin and Malinovsky, the Okhrana begin to make plans to split the Bolshevik party from within. When Malinovsky was instructed to set up a secret facility in Russia for printing subversive papers, the facility was quickly seized by the police and the people present arrested.

Likewise, wherever Malinovsky travelled inside Russia to meet with fellow Bolsheviks, arrests soon followed.

Obviously all these "coincidences" fueled rumors that Malinovsky was indeed a spy. However, Lenin remained unconvinced. In 1914, he wrote in Prosveshchenie:

> "Martov and Dan have long been known and repeatedly exposed as slanderers. This has been spoken of dozens of times in the press abroad....And after this, Martov and Dan want us to agree to an investigation undertaken on their initiative, on the basis of their slanderous statements, and with the participation of the very groups that shield them! That is downright impudence, and sheer stupidity on the part of the slanderers. We do not believe a single word of Dan's and Martov's. We shall never agree to any "investigation" into insidious rumours with the participation of the liquidators and the groups that help them. This would mean covering up the crime committed by Martov and Dan. We shall however thoroughly expose it to the working class."

Lenin even threatened those who brought their concerns to his attention with banishment from the party. When he and Nadya moved to Austria in 1913 to organize a special meeting of twenty-two Bolshevik leaders, at least five of those attending were actually Okhrana spies. Thus, those two close allies, along with his own arrogance and ignorance, worked together to help keep one of his worst enemies as his best friend.

Lenin also had other interests of a more personal nature. Though some historians still dispute it, Lenin allegedly took a mistress, Inessa Armand, a married woman with four children. As usual, Lenin focused on what he wanted rather than what society told him was morally right. Armand was bright, musical and a politically ardent member of the Bolsheviks who hung on Lenin's every word. There were even rumors that they had a child together, though that remains unproven.

Armand

In keeping with their open minded views of marriage and morality, Lenin told Nadya all about his relationship with Armand, and if this bothered her, she never admitted it. In fact, in her autobiographical story, *Reminisces on Lenin*, she spoke kindly of Inessa, adding that life "became cozier and gayer when Inessa came. Our entire life was filled with party concerns and affairs, more like a student commune than like family life, and we were glad to have Inessa... Something warm radiated from her talk."

Meanwhile, 1911 found Stalin living in St. Petersburg, where he soon became the editor of the new magazine, Pravda ("truth"). By now, in closer conformance with the goals of the Bolsheviks, Stalin had mostly dropped his focus on Georgian independence and revolution, partly because the area was dominated by Mensheviks. Though he would always retain his thick Georgian accent, Stalin finally began writing predominantly in Russian.

For the next year, Stalin would be part of the weekly paper, published legally at that time. Still, the government always kept a close eye on their articles and censored anything they did not like. In order to try to avoid censorship, the staff constantly renamed the paper, giving it a total eight different title in two years.

Unfortunately for Stalin, one of his fellow editors, Miron Chernomazov, was actually an undercover agent with the Russian police. His reports to his superiors led to Stalin's arrest in March of 1913 and subsequent exile for life to Siberia. As a result, he was out of the country for the most pivotal events of Russian Communist history, the capture and execution of Nicholas II and his family. How much the tales of this blood-bathed coup influenced Stalin's future crimes against humanity is unclear. However, the event did set the tone for how Russian leadership would deal with enemies of the state for the rest of the 20th century.

A government card from a file used to keep tabs on Stalin

Just as he had after his first sentencing, Trotsky managed to flee from Siberia carrying false papers and travel clandestinely to London. The exile community around the Social Democratic party that had thrived prior to 1905 was now dispersed somewhat by the chaos of the preceding years, but the party's fifth congress was convened in the summer of that year.

At that congress, the division between Martov's Menshevik faction and Lenin's Bolsheviks continued to widen, and the congress was the scene of ferocious debates between the rival groups. Each side accused the other of heresy and betrayal of the party's revolutionary commitment, and though Trotsky continued to remain neutral in the conflict, the general perception was that he was closer to the Mensheviks in outlook and approach. That perception had been reinforced by his work with the St. Petersburg Soviet, which operated in far greater agreement with Menshevik principles of openness and loose organization than with the Bolshevik approach of clandestine activity and tightly centralized control.

Subsequent to the 1907 congress, Trotsky made his way to Vienna, a move that placed him in the center of much of the intellectual and cultural ferment of the early 20th century. His closest collaborator there was fellow Russian Adolph Joffe, with whom he founded the highly influential socialist newspaper *Pravda* ("Truth"), which they would publish until 1912. Throughout the Vienna years, the sniping between the Bolsheviks and Mensheviks continued, but *Pravda* became Trotsky's latest attempt to be a voice of "non-factional" socialist politics. Not long after the paper was shut down, Lenin and his allies began to publish another *Pravda*, which went on to become the official Communist Party organ in the Soviet Union. Throughout this period, the Bolsheviks attempted to woo Trotsky to their side, probably because of the influence and popularity he had achieved as leader of the Soviet and editor of *Pravda*, but he remained independent.

Trotsky with his daughter Nina in 1915

Chapter 8: World War I

Perhaps because he was tired of living a double life, or maybe because of some desire for further adventure and fame, Malinovsky shocked Lenin and the other Bolsheviks by resigning from the Duma at the beginning of World War I and joining the Russian Army. He was wounded and captured the following year by the German Army and remained in a German Prisoner of War camp for the rest of the war. Still, Lenin forgave his old friend and continued to support him even as late as the end of 1916, when he reported that he felt sure Malinovsky regretted his rash move.

Malinovsky was hardly the only one who took to the fighting on behalf of his nation. Much to Lenin's chagrin, members of socialist parties across Europe rallied around their flags to support their countries, but Lenin felt that the war would be just one more example of poorer classes fighting the bourgeoisie's "imperialist war", instead of uniting together to engage in class warfare. In the year before the war broke out, Lenin asserted, "The bourgeoisie incites the workers of one nation against those of another in the endeavour to keep them disunited. Class-conscious workers, realising that the break-down of all the national barriers by capitalism is inevitable and progressive, are trying to help to enlighten and organise their fellow-workers from the backward countries."

When the war broke out, Lenin was living in Austria, one of the main belligerents of World War I and the one whose declaration of war on Serbia touched off the war after Archduke Franz

Ferdinand was assassinated. After a brief detention by authorities, Lenin headed to neutral Switzerland. Now secure in a neutral country, Lenin could give full voice to his opinions on the Great War. In 1916, Lenin published one of his best known books, *Imperialism: The Highest Stage of Capitalism*. In the book, Lenin argued that imperialistic empire was the final stage of capitalism and the source of the current war. Even worse, to Lenin Russia's participation was serving nobody's interests but the French and British, making Russia the poorer class and its allies the bourgeoise. Instead of retaining this status quo, Lenin encouraged all the Allied troops, not just the Russians, to turn around and fire on their own officers instead of the Germans.

Though Lenin opposed the war, at least in the manner it was being fought between belligerent nations, he also understood the opportunity the war provided. While many were calling for the Russians to pull out of the war entirely, especially as Russian loses mounted, Lenin called instead for the people to "turn the imperialist war into a civil war." He wanted the people of Russia to use the opportunity of a distracted monarchy to rise up and overthrow the Romanovs.

Ironically, his push for continuing the war brought him into conflict with many of his fellow socialists, particularly Rosa Luxemburg. She was quick to point out that socialism or even democracy would not protect the Russian people from the Germans, but Lenin nevertheless maintained, "International unity of the workers is more important than the national." When the International Socialist Burean Conference rolled around in Brussels in 1915, Lenin dispatched Inessa Armand to fight those who supported peace, including Luxemburg, Plekhanov, Trotsky and Martov. According to one historian, Lenin chose her instead of going himself because he trusted both her linguistic talent (she was fluent in five languages) and her loyalty to him.

Meanwhile, Trotsky left Zurich for Paris, but he was eventually deported by the French government, which was allied with Russia at the time and had no use for Russian revolutionaries. Trotsky was ultimately expelled from Europe altogether and put on an ocean liner heading to New York City.

Undeterred, Trotsky kept up his busy pace of activity on the other side of Atlantic, writing for radical newspapers and organizing Russian exiles, but he had not been in New York for three months before the news of revolution exploded once again out of Russia.

Chapter 9: The February Revolution, 1917

"The streets of Petrograd again speak the language of 1905. As in the time of the Russo-Japanese war, the masses demand bread, peace, and freedom. As in 1905, street cars are not running and newspapers do not appear. The workingmen let the steam out of the boilers, they quit their benches and walk out into the streets. The government mobilizes its Cossacks. And as was in 1905, only those two powers are facing each other in the streets – the revolutionary workingmen and the army of the Tzar." – Leon Trotsky, March 1917

Lenin's plan for a Russian Civil War received a catalyst from a strange place. In September of 1915, Tsar Nicholas II dismissed his generals on the Eastern Front and took over military command himself. Thus, as the number of battles lost grew, his reputation and popularity among the people fell. By 1917, it was clear that the Russian Army would never be able to sustain further involvement in the war, having already lost almost 8 million soldiers to death, injury and capture. With that, the Russian people began to cry out against the privations of the war. Factory workers staged strikes for higher wages to pay the ever inflating cost of food for their families. At the same time, people in Petrograd rioted in the streets, vandalizing shops and demanding food that the government simply did not have.

Had he been wiser, Nicholas might have appealed to the people, or met with the Duma to work out some sort of solution to the shortages. However, he had been raised with the understanding that the main work of a Tsar was to preserve the monarchy for his son. Thus, he decided on the very inopportune moment of late February, 1917 to try to disband the Duma and regain absolute power. When the Duma refused to disband, the High Commander of the army appealed to Nicholas, suggesting that he should abdicate before a full scale revolution broke out. Some suggested that the Tsar's cousin, Grand Duke Michael Alexandrovich would make an excellent replacement. He refused, however, and on March 1, Nicholas was forced to leave and was replaced with a Provisional Government which originally consisted of a mishmash of parliamentary figures and members of revolutionary councils that had been elected by workers, soldiers and peasants.

Lenin was still in exile in Zurich when the February Revolution pushed Nicholas II out of power, and he only found out about it on March 15. Understandably thrilled with this turn of events, Lenin began firing off missives to friends and allies in an attempt to harness the revolutionary energy and direct it toward an international class conflict, writing in one letter, "Spread out! Rouse new sections! Awaken fresh initiative, form new organisations in every stratum and prove to them that peace can come only with the armed Soviet of Workers' Deputies in power." At the same time, he and other members of the Provisional Government went about trying to secure his safe passage back to Russia, and eventually a Swiss colleague with contacts in the German Foreign Ministry was able to get Lenin a train ride into Russia. While that seems odd at first glance, it is apparent the German Foreign Ministry hoped that Lenin's agitation back in Russia would sufficiently distract the Russian Army and lead to their surrender to Germany or their quitting of the war.

The locomotive that brought Lenin back to Russia

Joining Lenin on his private train were 27 fellow Bolsheviks anxious to press forward the cause of socialism and shape the new political system. Passing through Germany, some passengers on the train were "struck by the total absence of grown-up men. Only women, teenagers and children could be seen at the wayside stations, on the fields, and in the streets of the towns." Lenin, however, was all about business. While on the train, he completed work on what became known as his famous April Theses, and he read them aloud as soon as he entered Petrograd on April 3rd. In it he outlined his plans for the immediate future:

1. In view of the undoubted honesty of the mass of rank and file representatives of revolutionary defencism who accept the war only as a necessity and not as a means of conquest,

in view of their being deceived by the bourgeoisie, it is necessary most thoroughly, persistently, patiently to explain to them their error, to explain the inseparable connection between capital and the imperialist war, to prove that without the overthrow of capital it is impossible to conclude the war with a really democratic, non-oppressive peace.

2. The peculiarity of the present situation in Russia is that it represents a transition from the first stage of the revolution - which, because of the inadequate organization and insufficient class-consciousness of the proletariat, led to the assumption of power by the bourgeoisie - to its second stage which is to place power in the hands of the proletariat and the poorest strata of the peasantry.

3. No support to the Provisional Government; exposure of the utter falsity of all its promises, particularly those relating to the renunciation of annexations. Unmasking, instead of admitting, the illusion-breeding "demand" that this government, a government of capitalist, should cease to be imperialistic.

4. Recognition of the fact that in most of the Soviets of Workers' Deputies our party constitutes a minority, and a small one at that, in the face of the bloc of all the petty bourgeois opportunist elements who have yielded to the influence of the bourgeoisie.

It must be explained to the masses that the Soviet of Workers' Deputies is the only possible form of revolutionary government and that, therefore, our task is, while this government is submitting to the influence of the bourgeoisie, to present a patient, systematic, and persistent analysis of its errors and tactics, an analysis especially adapted to the practical needs of the masses.

5. Not a parliamentary republic - a return to it from the Soviet of Workers' Deputies would be a step backward - but a republic of Soviets of Workers', Agricultural Labourers' and Peasants' Deputies throughout the land, from top to bottom.

Abolition of the police, the army, the bureaucracy. All officers to be elected and to be subject to recall at any time, their salaries not to exceed the average wage of a competent worker.

6. In the agrarian program, the emphasis must be shifted to the Soviets of Agricultural Laborers' Deputies [including]

    a. Confiscation of private lands.

    b. Nationalization of all lands in the country, and management of such lands by local Soviets of Agricultural Labourers' and Peasants' Deputies.

    c. A separate organization of Soviets of Deputies of the poorest peasants.

d. Creation of model agricultural establishments out of large estates.

7. Immediate merger of all the banks in the country into one general national bank, over which the Soviet of Workers' Deputies should have control.

8. Not the "introduction" of Socialism as an immediate task, but the immediate placing of the Soviet of Workers' Deputies in control of social production and distribution of goods.

9. Party tasks [include] Immediate calling of a party convention and Changing the party program, mainly:

a. Concerning imperialism and the imperialist war.

b. Concerning our attitude toward the state, and our demand for a 'commune state."

c. Amending our antiquated minimum program.

10. Rebuilding the International. Taking the initiative in the creation of a revolutionary International, an International against the social-chauvinists and against the "center".

Although the turmoil had been limited to Russia so far, and the Theses were written about how to immediately create a socialist state in Russia, it's clear that Lenin envisioned an international revolution even at this early date. As one historian characterized his thinking in 1917, "Lenin made his revolution for the sake of Europe, not for the sake of Russia, and he expected Russia's preliminary revolution to be eclipsed when the international revolution took place. Lenin did not invent the iron curtain."

Lenin's April Theses were among the most radical writings of his life to date, and both Mensheviks and fellow Bolsheviks were taken aback. The Theses were roundly condemned by the Mensheviks (one of whom described them as the "ravings of a madman"), and initially the Theses were supported by only one prominent Bolshevik, Alexandra Kollontai.

Kollontai

One of the people that were concerned about Lenin's insistence on an immediate revolution was Stalin. While he had always been fascinated by Lenin's ideals, he was usually too pragmatic to begin a venture without an assurance of success. Stalin had been in exile himself until returning to Siberia, and by April he was the editor of the popular Bolshevik paper *Pravda*. Stalin could not remain silent forever. Though Stalin and other Bolsheviks still believed that the revolution should be a bourgeoise revolution, the Theses at least presented a party platform and a banner under which revolutionaries could rally and united. Thus, after wrestling with the issue for ten days, Stalin wrote a scathing article supporting Lenin and urging the peasants to rise up immediately. He further instructed them to begin by forming local committees that would confiscate large, privately owned estates and turn them over to the peasants that worked on them. Even still, Lenin was going in an ideologically different direction, one that brought him closer to the political leanings of Trotsky.

Trotsky's journey from New York to Russia was slowed by a last-ditch effort to keep him out of Russia by detaining him in Nova Scotia, but he arrived in May 1917. In the months that followed, he developed a closer relationships with the Bolsheviks, who at the time were a relatively weak and marginal player in the chaotic political scene. Soon after, he was arrested under orders from Kerensky, who distrusted him because of his fiery leadership of the Soviet and clear involvement in Bolshevik plots to seize power. However, Trotsky was not held long, and when he was released, his ferocious criticism of the Provisional Government was successful in swaying the urban workers and soldiers toward the Bolshevik position. He was about to become indispensable to Lenin.

The chaos continued when Alexander Kerensky, the new head of the Provisional Government, launched yet another military offensive against the Germans in July of 1917. Soldiers deserted by the thousands, with many of them carrying their government issued weapons back to the estates where they lived. They often used these guns to threaten or even kill their landlords so that they could have their land. They also burned stately mansions and moved ancient boundary stones to create new, smaller farms for the peasants themselves to own.

Kerensky

Alarmed by the rioting and believing that it was a result of the impact Lenin and other revolutionaries were having on the common people, Kerensky outlawed the Bolsheviks and tried to round up its members, outlandishly accusing them of being German agents. Trotsky famously defended Lenin and other Bolsheviks against the charge, exhorting, "An intolerable atmosphere has been created, in which you, as well as we, are choking. They are throwing dirty accusations at Lenin and Zinoviev. Lenin has fought thirty years for the revolution. I have fought [for] twenty years against the oppression of the people. And we cannot but cherish a hatred for German militarism . . . I have been sentenced by a German court to eight months' imprisonment for my struggle against German militarism. This everybody knows. Let nobody in this hall say that we are hirelings of Germany." Luckily for Lenin, he got wind of the threat well enough ahead of time to escape to Finland, where he completed work on *State and Revolution*, an outline of the government he hoped to one day see in Russia.

Lenin in disguise in Finland, 1917

Chapter 10: Creating the Soviet Union

As the rioting was going on back at home, Kerensky's July Offensive failed miserably, and he came into conflict with his new general, Lavr Kornilov, over policies related to discipline and production. When Kornilov sent the troops under his command to march on Kerensky's headquarters in Petrograd, Kerensky had to appeal to the Bolsheviks for Red Guards to protect his capitol city. Lenin reluctantly agreed and immediately recruited more than 25,000 soldiers to protect the government he so vehemently opposed. When Kornilov's troops saw the rows of dug in Red Guards, they refused to advance, and Kornilov surrendered to the palace police.

Realizing that he now had the Provisional Government largely at his mercy, Lenin returned to Russia in October and set up a party headquarters in Smolny Institute for Girls in St. Petersburg. From there, he quietly ordered that the Provisional Government be deposed and the Winter Palace vacated. On the evening of October 25, the Second All-Russian Congress of Soviets met at the Smolny Institute to establish a new government. While there were initially some disagreements over the overthrow of the Provisional Government, Martov's Mensheviks and Lenin's Bolsheviks eventually agreed to share power. Ironically, after all the drama that had surrounded the earlier months of that year, the October Revolution went largely unnoticed. As

Lenin had written a month earlier, "The peaceful development of any revolution is, generally speaking, extremely rare and difficult ... but ... a peaceful development of the revolution is possible and probable if all power is transferred to the Soviets. The struggle of parties for power within the Soviets may proceed peacefully, if the Soviets are made fully democratic." It seemed that way in October.

Lenin arrived at the meeting the next evening to thunderous applause, appearing without a disguise for the first time since July. Famous American journalist John Reed, who would later chronicle the Russian Revolution in his critically acclaimed book, *Ten Days That Shook The World*, described Lenin for readers. "A short, stocky figure, with a big head set down in his shoulders, bald and bulging. Little eyes, a snubbish nose, wide, generous mouth, and heavy chin; clean-shaven now, but already beginning to bristle with the well-known beard of his past and future. Dressed in shabby clothes, his trousers much too long for him. Unimpressive, to be the idol of a mob, loved and revered as perhaps few leaders in history have been. A strange popular leader—a leader purely by virtue of intellect; colourless, humourless, uncompromising and detached, without picturesque idiosyncrasies—but with the power of explaining profound ideas in simple terms, of analysing a concrete situation. And combined with shrewdness, the greatest intellectual audacity."

Beginning his speech with "We shall now proceed to construct the Socialist order!", at the meeting, Lenin proposed a "Decree on Peace" calling for an end of the war, and a "Decree on Land" announcing that all property owned by large land owners and the aristocracy would be given to the peasants. Both decrees passed with little dissension. Next, the new government elected a Bolshevik majority to the Council of People's Commissars, with the Mensheviks joining the government a few weeks later. Lenin was soon elected Chairman of the Council, making him head of the government, though he had originally intended for the position to go to Trotsky, who declined because he worried his Jewish ethnicity would pose problems.

In recognition of his contribution, the now totally empowered Lenin appointed Stalin the Commissar of Nationalities, joking with him about his meteoric rise to power. As Commissar, Stalin was in charge of all the non-Russian people in the country, including Buriats, Byelorussians, Georgians, Tadzhiks, Ukrainians and Yakuts, nearly half the country's population. The spoiled little boy who'd been forced to speak Russian and had been teased about his appearance was now a bitter, angry man with nearly unlimited power. The combination would not make for a pretty outcome.

Initially, however, it looked like all would be well for these foreigners under Russian control. He concluded his famous Helsinki address of 1917 with these words of encouragement and promises of support:

"Comrades! Information has reached us that your country is experiencing approximately the same crisis of power as Russia experienced on the eve of the October

Revolution. Information has reached us that attempts are being made to frighten you too with the bogey of famine, sabotage, and so on. Permit me to tell you on the basis of the practical experience of the revolutionary movement in Russia that these dangers, even if real, are by no means insuperable! These dangers can be overcome if you act resolutely and without faltering. In the midst of war and economic disruption, in the midst of the revolutionary movement which is flaring up in the West and of the increasing victories of the workers' revolution in Russia, there are no dangers or difficulties that could withstand your onslaught. In such a situation only one power, socialist power, can maintain itself and conquer. In such a situation only one kind of tactics can be effective, the tactics of Danton—audacity, audacity and again audacity! And if you should need our help, you will have it—we shall extend you a fraternal hand. Of this you may rest assured."

Unfortunately, the non-Russian peoples who heard or read this speech remained unconvinced. They were not so much interested in Russian help as they were national determination. Therefore they proved to be a constant source of stress to the new Commissar, setting up their own governments, opposing Bolshevik policy, and overall acting with the self-determination they had been promised, as long as they determined to join the new Union of Soviet Socialist Republics.

Faced with this level of opposition to his and the other Bolsheviks' plans, Stalin took a different tact. Accusing the new independent governments of being under the control of "the bourgeoisie," he agreed with Lenin that a more centralized government was needed. As the Russian Civil War played out during the early 1920s, Stalin became more involved in military matters while Lenin continued to focus on politics.

Trotsky, meanwhile, had become chairman of the Petrograd Soviet in St. Petersburg (which had its name changed to Petrograd during World War I to sound less German). Trotsky regained his reputation as a fiery and charismatic speaker with great sway over the city's working class. At the same time, during and after his prison stint, he solidified his relations with the Bolsheviks and Lenin and finally joined the party, ending his status as a factionless coalition-builder and severing his earlier ties to the Mensheviks, who had been allied with Kerensky's governing coalition.

Having seen how easily a multi-generational dynasty fell, Lenin was obviously concerned about keeping his own infant administration safe. To this end, he established "The Whole-Russian Extraordinary Commission for Combating Counter-Revolution and Sabotage" in the last weeks of 1917. Known colloquially as the Cheka (Extraordinary Commission), it soon became as feared by non-socialists as the Tsar's secret police had ever been. In addition to monitoring the movements of anyone opposing the government, the Cheka also enforced censorship laws against non-socialist newspapers.

Trotsky's immediate role after the revolution was Commissar of Foreign Affairs, and specifically his task was to negotiate the end of the devastating war with Germany, which had been a key Bolshevik promise throughout the war. Still, Trotsky had to walk a narrow line, particularly because he did not wish to provide aid or support to the reactionary Kaiser's government in Germany. In fact, Trotsky and the other Bolsheviks had long hoped that the German workers would be inspired by events in Russia and then rise up and spread the revolution across enemy lines.

While Lenin wanted Russia out of the war, he initially hoped to retain the land it had lost to the Germans. He worked with Trotsky to formulate a Russo-German treaty in which each country would agree to return any land gained from the other during the war. When this failed, he had to concede much of the Russian countryside to the Germans in return for pulling the Russians out of the war. The Treaty of Brest-Litovsk officially removed Russia from the conflict on March 3, 1918. However, it also resulted in Germany being so close to Petrograd that the government had to move its capital to Moscow.

Lenin and Fritz Platten

In spite of the Cheka's best efforts, those who opposed Lenin and the Bolsheviks were still out there, and they were gunning for Lenin, literally. In January 1918, gunmen shot at Lenin and Fritz Platten as they sat in an automobile after Lenin had given a speech, which Lenin survived after Platten pushed him down and shielded him. But the most famous assassination attempt would come in August 1918, when a supporter of the Socialist Revolutionary Party, Fanya Kaplan, approached Lenin as he sat in an automobile. After calling to him to get his attention, she fired at him three times, hitting him once in the arm and once in the jaw and neck. Though the wounds rendered him unconscious, Lenin survived the shooting, and fearful of people at the hospital who might try to finish the job, he returned to the Kremilin and ordered physicians to come there to treat him where he felt safe. Ultimately, doctors refused to perform surgery given the precarious position of the bullet in his neck. Pravda used the attempt for propaganda purposes, reporting, "Lenin, shot through twice, with pierced lungs spilling blood, refuses help and goes on his own. The next morning, still threatened with death, he reads papers, listens, learns, and observes to see that the engine of the locomotive that carries us towards global revolution has not stopped working..."

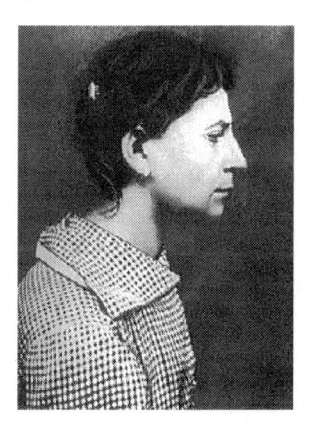

Fanya Kaplan

Despite that, Soviet officials began to downplay the attack, and many across Russia never learned of it. Though he survived the attack, the bullets were left in place and continued to erode his health. However, Lenin kept working and appearing in public, determined to keep the public ignorant of how weak his condition was becoming. This was important because Lenin was increasingly viewed as the embodiment of the new regime, and it was feared that his death could cause everything to crumble. One former Tsarist wrote as much, reporting after the attempt, "As it happens, the attempt to kill Lenin has made him much more popular than he was. One hears a great many people, who are far from having any sympathy with the Bolsheviks, saying that it would be an absolute disaster if Lenin had succumbed to his wounds, as it was first thought he would. And they are quite right, for, in the midst of all this chaos and confusion, he is the backbone of the new body politic, the main support on which everything rests.."

The Bolsheviks may have downplayed the assassination attempt publicly, but they were privately plotting retaliation on a massive scale. Two weeks before Kaplan's attempt on Lenin's life, the Petrograd Cheka chief Moisei Uritsky had been assassinated, and now Stalin suggested to Lenin that they should engage in "open and systematic mass terror…[against] those responsible." Thus, the Cheka, under the instruction of Stalin, launched what later came to be known as the "Red Terror" in response to the assassination attempt. In the weeks that followed, more than 800 people were executed, including the entire Romanov family. This however, was just the beginning. As the Bolsheviks, known popularly as the Red Russians fought an ongoing war against those who opposed socialism (the White Russians), more than 18,000 people were executed on charges related to opposing Lenin and his rule. While historians have often debated the extent of Lenin's personal involvement in the executions, Trotsky himself later asserted that it was Lenin who authorized the execution of the Russian Royal Family.

Though he is often remembered as a vocal opponent of Stalin's terror (and ultimately a victim of it), Trotsky was fully in support of the Cheka's methods and even took time to write and publish a full-throated defense of them in the book *Terrorism and Communism* (1920). He also defended the policies of "War Communism," including large-scale confiscation of produce, livestock, and grains in order to fuel the war effort, practices that placed a devastating burden on the rural poor in particular. Trotsky summed up his defense of all of these measures in *Terrorism and Communism*:

> "The more perfect the revolution, the greater are the masses it draws in; and the longer it is prolonged, the greater is the destruction it achieves in the apparatus of production, and the more terrible inroads does it make upon public resources. From this there follows merely the conclusion which did not require proof – that a civil war is harmful to economic life. But to lay this at the door of the Soviet economic system is like accusing a new-born human being of the birth-pangs of the mother who brought him into the world."

Victims of the Red Terror

Almost immediately after pulling Russia out of World War I, Trotsky found himself in charge of an equally daunting task: organizing the defense of the Bolshevik revolutionary state against the many enemies who had sprung up in succeeding months. These enemies, including Tsarists, liberals, and anti-Bolshevik leftists, all arrayed in violent and intractable opposition, often with significant foreign support. The Bolsheviks initially counted on a spontaneous campaign of support from the working classes, but the organizational weaknesses of their loyal force, the Red Guard, soon displayed themselves. Trotsky was placed in charge of organizing the new Red Army that would defend the fragile revolutionary state against foes both native and foreign. Just after peace had been settled in Germany, it was time again to prepare for war.

Bolshevik propaganda depicting Trotsky as St. George slaying a dragon with the word counterrevolutionary on it.

Trotsky's placement at the helm of the Red Army was a surprising choice, given that he had no military experience and all of his battles up to that point had taken place in print, but if the Bolsheviks' enemies expected they would have little to fear from a force under the command of an intellectual with no training in war, they soon found themselves mistaken. Trotsky's overnight transformation into a brilliant martial tactician was perhaps paralleled in the 20th century only by that of fellow Marxist Che Guevara, who would go from asthmatic physician to effective guerrilla leader during the Cuban Revolution a generation later. To be fair, however, part of Trotsky's success in charge of the army resulted from his decision to recruit former Tsarist generals into leadership positions. This move was controversial among the Bolshevik leadership, which had little trust for anyone associated with the old regime, but Trotsky had recognized that the fierce commitment of Bolshevik recruits would be insufficient for the Red Army to stand its own against the many forces now assembled against it. The Tsarist officers were also recruited for their expertise and experience were monitored closely to ensure their continued loyalty by the newly created commissars, who enforced ideological purity.

Trotsky also instilled discipline in his forces through fear, which he believed was a necessary ingredient. In his autobiography, Trotsky asserted:

> "An army cannot be built without reprisals. Masses of men cannot be led to death unless the army command has the death-penalty in its arsenal. So long as those malicious tailless apes that are so proud of their technical achievements—the animals that we call men—will build armies and wage wars, the command will always be obliged to place the soldiers between the possible death in the front and the inevitable one in the rear. And yet armies are not built on fear. The Tsar's army fell to pieces not because of any lack of reprisals. In his attempt to save it by restoring the death-penalty, Kerensky only finished it. Upon the ashes of the great war, the Bolsheviks created a new army. These facts demand no explanation for any one who has even the slightest knowledge of the language of history. The strongest cement in the new army was the ideas of the October revolution, and the train supplied the front with this cement."

At the same time, Trotsky still believed in the power of persuasion, and he sought to bring back deserters by appealing to their revolutionary instincts. He noted:

> "In the provinces of Kaluga, Voronezh, and Ryazan, tens of thousands of young peasants had failed to answer the first recruiting summons by the Soviets ... The war commissariat of Ryazan succeeded in gathering in some fifteen thousand of such deserters. While passing through Ryazan, I decided to take a look at them. Some of our men tried to dissuade me. 'Something might happen,' they warned me. But everything went off beautifully. The men were called out of their barracks. 'Comrade-deserters – come to the meeting. Comrade Trotsky has come to speak to you.' They ran out excited, boisterous, as curious as schoolboys. I had imagined them much worse, and they had imagined me as more terrible. In a few minutes, I was surrounded by a huge crowd of unbridled, utterly undisciplined, but not at all hostile men. The 'comrade-deserters' were looking at me with such curiosity that it seemed as if their eyes would pop out of their heads. I climbed on a table there in the yard, and spoke to them for about an hour and a half. It was a most responsive

audience. I tried to raise them in their own eyes; concluding, I asked them to lift their hands in token of their loyalty to the revolution. The new ideas infected them before my very eyes. They were genuinely enthusiastic; they followed me to the automobile, devoured me with their eyes, not fearfully, as before, but rapturously, and shouted at the tops of their voices. They would hardly let me go. I learned afterward, with some pride, that one of the best ways to educate them was to remind them: 'What did you promise Comrade Trotsky?' Later on, regiments of Ryazan 'deserters' fought well at the fronts."

Trotsky reviewing soldiers in 1919

The forces of the so-called White Army, made up of anti-Bolshevik Russians of all stripes, and their allies from nearly all the major European nations, combined to place the new revolutionary regime in a state of siege. In response, the Bolsheviks introduced a number of policies that would set the stage for the state terrorism and suppression of later years.

White Army propaganda poster depicting Trotsky as Satan

Unfortunately, bullets weren't all that was killing the Russian common people. While the Whites and Reds engaged in a civil war that would last for nearly 7 years, ordinary Russians were starving due to war time communism measures that allowed the Soviet government to confiscate food for soldiers from peasant farms with little or no payment. When the farmers retaliated by growing fewer crops, the Cheka responded by executing or imprisoning the offending peasants. However, even the Cheka could not cause plants to grow, and during the Famine of 1921, more than 5 million Russians starved to death in and near their own homes. This tragedy, along with the civil unrest it provoked, led Lenin to institute the New Economic Policy to rejuvenate the both agriculture and industry.

In formulating his economic policies, Lenin asserted, "We must show the peasants that the organisation of industry on the basis of modern, advanced technology, on electrification, which will provide a link between town and country, will put an end to the division between town and country, will make it possible to raise the level of culture in the countryside and to overcome, even in the most remote corners of land, backwardness, ignorance, poverty, disease, and barbarism." Of course, to Lenin that meant total State control over industry, and he implemented a system in which every industry was overseen by one ruling official granted all the deciding power over any disputes, thereby completely curbing workers' self-management rights.

A propagandist picture that reads, "Comrade Lenin Cleanses the Earth of Filth"

Lenin's first non-political interest was in bringing electricity to all of Russia, so that the homes and factories could be modernized. Disappointed with the lack of progress made by factories under their own power, Lenin made the first of many moves to expand government control over private lives by placing businesses under the supervision of Soviet committees. These committees would evaluate everything from worker rights to productivity to the flow of materials. They would then report to the government, who would, it was hoped, take steps to help the factories improve their productivity.

Having established a plan for economic improvements, Lenin turned his attention to social issues. First, he instituted a system of free health care for all Russians, as well as a widespread system of public education. With the encouragement of both his wife and his mistress, he encouraged the government to grant women the right to vote, and to encourage them to take advantage of higher education to train to enter the work force.

Chapter 11: Stalin and the Russian Civil War

Like Trotsky, Stalin also cut his teeth in the Russian Civil War, and his military strategy was as effective as it was ruthless. Prior to his successful battle against the White Army at Tsaritsyn, he met with the local leaders on a boat tied up along the shore of the Volga River. It is rumored that he interviewed them thoroughly and then sent the ones he believed to be loyal back to their homes and offices. The ones whose loyalty he questioned were summarily shot and thrown in the river.

Stalin's desire for blood had been fed by the assassination of Moisei Uritsky and the attempt on the life of Lenin himself in August, 1918. In a telegram to the badly wounded Lenin on August 31, Stalin committed himself to revenge:

> "Having learned of the villainous attempt of the hirelings of the bourgeoisie on the life of Comrade Lenin, the world's greatest revolutionary and the tried and tested leader and teacher of the proletariat, the Military Council of the North Caucasian Military Area is answering this vile attempt at assassination by instituting open and systematic mass terror against the bourgeoisie and its agents."

Lenin passed Stalin's recommendation on to Felix Dzerzhinsky, the head of Soviet state security, who in turn instituted the famous Red Terror the next day. The unintended consequence of this genocide was that the Bolsheviks government became increasingly unpopular with the common Russian people. While they supported the ideas of freedom and brotherhood in general, they were not terribly sanguine about seeing more and more people around them hauled from their homes and shot. Many could sense the mania in the air and they wanted no part of it.

Following the Kronstadt Uprising in which Soviet military men and civilians teamed up to call for an end to the random slaughter of their countrymen, Lenin loosened up the government's control on economic policy. He even instituted the New Economic Policy, which allowed farmers to once again sell their produce in local markets. Those who needed to could even employ others to work for them without falling under the suspicion of being wealthy landowners. Those who did not farm were also allowed more freedom to own and run private businesses, including small factories.

While Stalin agreed with the New Economic Policy, others did not, and fighting to keep it alive began to take its toll of Lenin's health. Thus, in April of 1922, he met with other party leaders and asked that Stalin be appointed the first General Secretary of the Soviet Union. One of Stalin's powers as General Secretary allowed him to dismiss any party members he deemed useless or disloyal. Coincidentally, he quickly discovered the most of the followers of his arch rival, Leon Trotsky, fell into this category. Therefore, he was able to remove from party participation thousands of otherwise loyal members. He replaced them with members whom he knew to be loyal to him, and whose continued loyalty he could count on, since their comfortable positions depended on it.

No one thought much of this move since Lenin appeared to still be in complete charge of the party, and it passed with little discussion. However, when Lenin suffered a stroke a few months later and was left paralyzed, either Trotsky or Stalin seemed to be the next in line.

Chapter 12: Lenin's Death

Throughout all this time, Lenin remained in increasingly poor health due to the bullets still in his body, as well as the fact that he was working upwards of 14-16 hours per day running the new nation. Russian historian Dmitri Volkogonov famously described a typical work day for the premier: "Lenin was involved in the challenges of delivering fuel into Ivanovo-Vosnesensk... the provision of clothing for miners, he was solving the question of dynamo construction, drafted dozens of routine documents, orders, trade agreements, was engaged in the allocation of rations, edited books and pamphlets at the request of his comrades, held hearings on the applications of peat, assisted in improving the workings at the "Novii Lessner" factory, clarified in correspondence with the engineer P. A. Kozmin the feasibility of using wind turbines for the electrification of villages... all the while serving as an adviser to party functionaries almost continuously."

Lenin working in the Kremlin, 1918

In April of 1922, doctors finally decided to remove the bullet in Lenin's neck, but after a month spent resting and recovering, Lenin returned to his grueling schedule. This proved to be too much for his fragile physical state and he suffered a stroke just a month later. Though it affected his speech and his movement on the right side, he began to gradually recover by June and made the imprudent choice of going back to work. In addition to resuming duties in August, he also delivered a series of long speeches in November.

Lenin and Stalin after Lenin's first stroke

Even as Trotsky's Red Army was successfully beating back the advances of the White Army, he was becoming embroiled in the conflicts that would ultimately bring about his political demise. By 1921, it was clear that Lenin's health was deteriorating rapidly, and those in the inner circles of the Bolshevik leadership began to contemplate their leader's succession. Trotsky was at once Lenin's most visible ally and therefore his most likely successor, but he was an object of suspicion among other members of the Bolshevik Central Committee because he had not joined the party until the middle of 1917. Conversely, most of the others had stood with Lenin's faction from the beginning of the split with the Mensheviks, including Stalin, a less publicly known but increasingly significant player with whom Trotsky sparred over tactical issues throughout the Civil War period and after.

After the first stroke, weakened by his physical condition, Lenin fell prey to Stalin's ambition. In October of 1922, the Central Committee voted to accept Stalin's foreign trade policy instead of the one put forward by Lenin. Seeing the handwriting on the wall, Lenin contacted Trotsky and suggested that they team up to try to hold Stalin in check. Trotsky agreed, and together they saw Stalin's policy overturned at the next committee meeting.

Unfortunately for Lenin, he had employed Stalin's wife, Nadya, as his secretary. She found a copy of the letter he sent to Trotsky and shared its contents with her husband. He in turn called Lenin's wife, Nadezhda, and berated her over the phone for allowing her weak and obviously delusional husband to write such a letter. This phone call sealed Stalin's fate in Lenin's eyes, and he dictated a letter in which he suggested that Stalin was not fit to take his place as the party's leader.

Sensing death was coming after the first stroke, Lenin began dictating instructions on how he would like the Soviet government to be continued, comprising what came to be known as Lenin's Testament near the end of 1922. In addition to dictating how the Soviet government should be structured, it was particularly notable in its criticism of several high-ranking officials, including Stalin, Trotsky, Grigory Zinoviev, Lev Kamenev, and Nikolai Bukharin. Lenin was extremely concerned about Stalin, who had become Communist Party's General Secretary in 1922. In it he compared Stalin negatively to Trotsky, saying,

> "Comrade Stalin, having become General Secretary, has concentrated an enormous power in his hands; and I am not sure that he always knows how to use that power with sufficient caution. On the other hand, Comrade Trotsky, as was proved by his struggle against the Central Committee in connection with the question of the People's Commissariat of Ways and Communications, is distinguished not only by his exceptional abilities – personally he is, to be sure, the most able man in the present Central Committee – but also by his too far-reaching self-confidence and a disposition to be too much attracted by the purely administrative side of affairs."

Lenin completed this letter on Christmas Day, 1922. However, a few days later, perhaps concerned that he had not made his concerns sufficiently clear, he added the following post-script.

> "Stalin is too rude, and this fault, entirely supportable in relations among us Communists, becomes insupportable in the office of General Secretary. Therefore, I propose to the comrades to find a way to remove Stalin from that position and appoint to it another man who in all respects differs from Stalin only in superiority – namely, more patient, more loyal, more polite and more attentive to comrades, less capricious, etc. This circumstance may seem an insignificant trifle, but I think that from the point of view of preventing a split and from the point of view of the relation between Stalin and Trotsky which I discussed above, it is not a trifle, or it is such a trifle as may acquire a decisive significance."

Lenin simply burned his body out by continuing to push it to its physical limits, and he suffered a second stroke in December of that same year, which partly paralyzed the right side of his body. The third and final stroke in March of 1923 proved his final undoing, rendering him mute and bedridden.

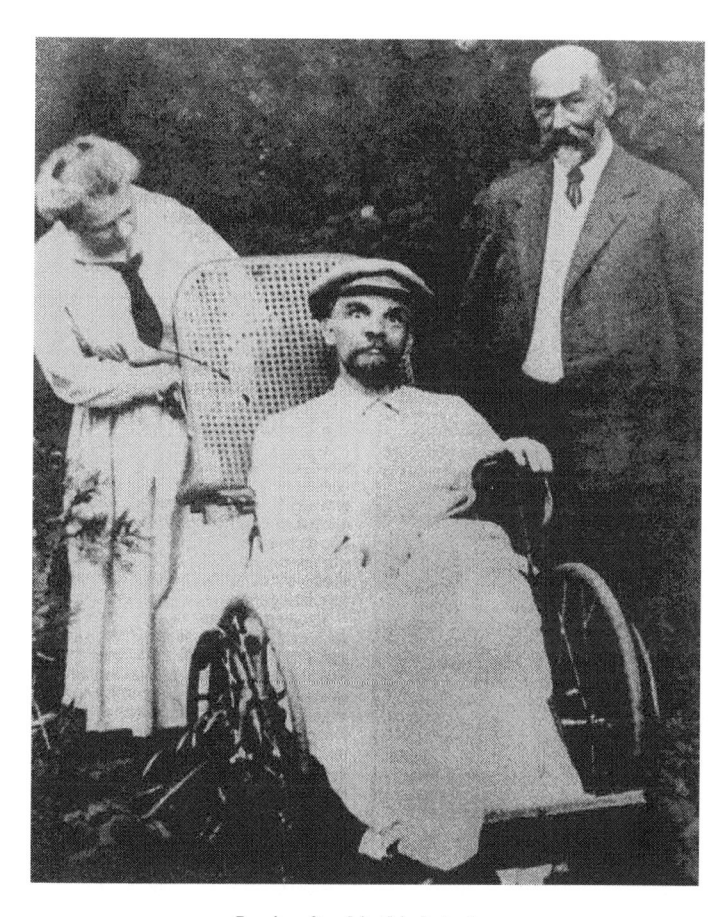

Lenin after his third stroke

Site of Lenin's death

On January 21, 1924, Lenin's body finally gave out, and he died that night in his estate at Gorki at just 53 years old. For four days his body lay in state, during which time nearly a million mourners passed through to see it. By then, Petrograd had been renamed Leningrad. Most famously, Lenin's body was embalmed and placed for public display in Lenin's Mausoleum, where plenty of visitors can still pass by his body and view it each day. It is estimated that over 100 million have viewed his body in the last 88 years.

Pallbearers carrying Lenin's coffin

Chapter 13: Stalin Comes to Power

Throughout the period of Lenin's illness and the successful winding down of the Civil War, the issues that had divided the Mensheviks and the Bolsheviks two decades before reemerged as subjects of practical debate. First of all, there was an economic debate about whether the confiscatory policies of "War Communism" should continue. The Bolsheviks had to decide whether to move the country rapidly toward a communistic model of production as envisioned by Marx, or whether there should be a loosening of restrictions on economic activity in order to foster and incentivize a resurgence of production after many harsh years of war. The latter proposal proceeded from the old assumption that the under-industrialized Soviet economy was not yet ready for the transition to full-scale socialism, and therefore needed to undergo further capitalistic development with this ultimate goal in mind. In part because of the strikes and uprisings provoked by the harsh regime of "War Communism," the Bolshevik leadership ultimately acceded to this more liberalized regime, dubbed the "New Economic Policy."

A second question reprised in these years was the question of how centralized the party, and therefore the state, should be. Should trade unions and other workers' organizations be able to obtain some autonomy? Trotsky, who took charge of rebuilding the national railways after the end of the Civil War, initially argued against trade union autonomy, but soon after that he came to criticize the increasing concentration of power among the party's inner circle. Of course, that concentration of power was being led by Stalin in his capacity as General Secretary of the party, and it was accepted by his allies Kamenev and Zinoviev.

The factional struggles of the Bolsheviks in the 1920's make for a convoluted story, but they can be understood as ideological struggles over how to implement communism and personal struggles between highly ambitious men. The splits within the party continued the fundamental questions about party organization that divided the Bolsheviks from their opponents in the first place. Stalin and his allies opted for a model of highly concentrated and centralized power wielded by a small revolutionary vanguard, while Trotsky and the so-called Left Opposition advocated a greater openness and pluralism advanced through the democratic institution of the Soviets. This is not to say that Trotsky took a more tolerant view of opposition to the Bolshevik agenda; he had personally advocated the persecution of Mensheviks, Social Revolutionaries, and other rivals on the left, consigning them in one famous speech to the "dustbin of history." But the more Trotsky saw of the concentration of power in the hands of a new governing elite, the more wary he became.

At the same time, the ideological affiliations of both Trotsky and Stalin in this period seem to have been partially strategic. Each assumed their respective positions at least in part to attempt to position themselves against the other in what was emerging as an epic battle of will. Trotsky recognized the battle lines being drawn as early as 1919, noting, "It is no wonder that my military work created so many enemies for me. I did not look to the side, I elbowed away those who interfered with military success, or in the haste of the work trod on the toes of the unheeding and was too busy even to apologize. Some people remember such things. The dissatisfied and those whose feelings had been hurt found their way to Stalin or Zinoviev, for these two also nourished hurts."

Lenin was the unquestioned head of the new Soviet Union, and upon his death he had firmly expressed the desire to make sure Stalin didn't concentrate power and control over the young Communist nation. Of course, that's precisely what ended up happening. So how and why did Lenin's Testament go unheeded?

Trotsky was in the faraway Caucasus when Lenin finally died in the beginning of 1924, and he reacted by writing, "And now Vladimir Ilyich is no more. The party is orphaned. The workmen's class is orphaned. This was the very feeling aroused by the news of the death of our teacher and leader." But Stalin and his allies took advantage of their rival's absence to suppress documents written by Lenin shortly before his death that pleaded for the reconciliation of the factions. They also used the absence of Trotsky from the leader's funeral as an opportunity to resurrect insinuations about his loyalty.

When Lenin's widow unearthed the document for Soviet officials, it was quickly disregarded and suppressed by Stalin, Kamenev, and Zinoviev, the ruling troika that Lenin had disparaged. Other leaders also went about making sure the Testament had no effect, including Trotsky, who published an article countering its importance and asserting that they were not a will and had not technically been violated. It was a stance Trotsky himself would come to regret in ensuing years as his opposition to Stalin increased.

While the letter made clear Lenin's intentions, it did not have the force of law behind it, especially with the remaining Soviet leaders asserting that it was not a final will. Since Lenin died before he could use his own personal leadership to enforce his wishes, Stalin became the preeminent Soviet leader. At the same time, his battle with Lenin had given him a sense of the bigger picture, and he now saw the wisdom of moving more slowly, especially when dealing with the common people. Therefore, he initially left the New Economic Policy in place and even allowed the farmers to buy up land around them to expand their farms. These larger landowners were known at kulaks, meaning "fists" for the tight way in which they held on to their land.

On the political front, Stalin had other things on his mind. As the General Secretary of the Soviet Union, he courted the favor of Lev Kamenev and Grigory Zinoviev, two powerful members of the Politburo, to keep Trotsky in check. He encouraged rumors that Trotsky would probably oust them if he came to power so that he could put his own people in power. He also encouraged a sense of his superiority, along with theirs, against the upstart Trotsky, who hadn't even joined the party until 1917.

Kamenev

Zinoviev

    Trotsky initially thought he had an ace in the hole: Lenin's last letter. In 1924, he persuaded Lenin's widow to demand its publication. However, Zinoviev was one step ahead of him and made an impassioned speech indicating that the great leader's fears had been unfounded, since the party had prospered so well under Stalin's leadership. Since a majority of the members of the Central Committee had been appointed by Stalin himself, they quickly agreed that Zinoviev was right and the letter remained unpublished.

Heady with the success of once again standing down his old enemy, Stalin moved in for the kill. In 1925, he worked with his allies on the Central Committee to have Trotsky removed from office. Though his supporters urged him to fight the decision, with arms if necessary, Trotsky had had enough of politics and agreed to resign quietly.

As soon as he no longer needed their help against Trotsky, Stalin began to speak openly against Kamenev and Zinoviev. He attacked Trotsky's position that the role of the Soviet Union should be to spread communism throughout the world, a position also held by Zinoviev and Kamenev. Instead, he maintained that it was more important to solidify and maintain power within the states of the Soviet Union. This put Kamenev and Zinoviev in an awkward position, since they didn't want to oppose a powerful ally and come to agree with a man they had just helped depose.

Since Zinoviev and Kamenev seemed unlikely to continue to support Trotsky, Stalin felt secure enough to turn his political attention to other members of the Central Committee. However, the men soon overcame their embarrassment about their past attacks on Trotsky and finally publically joined forces with him against Stalin in 1926. By that time, however, it was too late. Stalin, accusing them of promoting disharmony and disunity, had them thrown off the Central Committee. Since a political split into a two party system was among the Soviet Union's greatest fears, Zinoviev and Kamenev agreed to resign quietly. Trotsky, on the other hand, made no such promises and was banished to Kazakhstan.

Ironically, when Trotsky was expelled from a Communist Party now thoroughly dominated by Stalin in 1927, his old enemy Zinoviev was expelled alongside him. Now disempowered but still enjoying popular support, Trotsky was far too dangerous for Stalin to allow to remain in the country. He was sent into exile for the third and final time through Russia's southwestern border with Turkey.

Trotsky's home in Istanbul, Turkey

Chapter 14: Industrial Modernization

With his political position secured, Stalin turned his attention toward his country's economic situation. In order to make the farms across the Soviet Union produce enough food to feed the ever expanding population, Stalin learned that the farmers would need 250,000 new, gas powered tractors. Not only did these need to be built, but they would need to be powered, so he also had to find a way to pump and refine the extensive oil deposits lying underground in much of the northern regions of the country. Finally, farms needed electricity, which meant more power plants and wires strung across great distances.

In order to accomplish this, Stalin had to get more factories up and running. They had just barely gotten back to their pre-Revolution level of production, much less seen any growth. However, he was determined, and brought the same force that he had already used against the Politburo to bear on the factories. To this end, he created and enforced in 1928 the first of many Five Year Plans.

He began by going after the kulaks. They tended to grow and sell food near their own homes and villages, while he wanted more produce imported into the cities to feed the factory workers and their families. Therefore, in 1928 he began pressuring them to abandon their independent farms and join together as collectives.

Not surprisingly, Stalin's promises of higher production and better profits largely fell on deaf ears. Though he tried to explain that, as part of a cooperative, the farmers could pool their resources and buy better equipment, the men and women who had worked the same land for generations were less than enthusiastic. This did not please Stalin at all, and perhaps even stirred up memories of the peasants who had teased him as a young boy. They definitely stood for all that he had tried to put behind him when he left Gori for the big city.

Frustration often brings out the worst in people, and this was so for Stalin. He ordered his underlings on the local level to take possession of the kulak's land and have them gathered together into state owned collective farms. Those who resisted were shot out right, including thousands of kulak farmers and their families. Furthermore, anyone else who got in his way was sent to Siberia or Russian holdings in Central Asia. According to Soviet records, about 1 in 4 failed to survive the trip.

At the same time Stalin was also determined to see growth in factory output. He set goals for tremendous increases in the production of coal, iron and electricity. He spread rumors that, if these goals were not met, the Soviet Union would be in danger of eminent invasion. He also encouraged factory managers to set goals for their workers and to publically ostracize those that did not meet them.

Discouraged by insurmountable demands, many workers simply stopped coming in for work. If this became a pattern for an individual, he would be arrested and charged with sabotage by not working hard enough to support the Five Year Plan. If deemed guilty, the worker could be sent to a forced labor camp, either on the dreaded Siberian Railway or along the Baltic Sea Canal. The worst offenders were shot outright as a warning to others.

To be fair, Stalin did not only authorize threats and punishments to motivate workers. He also pushed the Central Committee to offer higher wages to those who excelled. Committee members argued against what they saw as a betrayal of the egalitarian principles of the revolution, but in the end Stalin prevailed, and by the early 1930s those who developed the necessary skills to serve the good of the people could expect to be rewarded with higher wages.

Though his he had won the battle for higher wages, Stalin was in grave danger of losing the war over control of the Politburo. By the summer of 1932, opposition to his policies had risen to such a fevered pitch that members were calling for his expulsion and the reinstatement of Leon Trotsky to power. Not surprisingly, Stalin met this threat aggressively and demanded that those who dared criticize him should be rounded up and shot. At this, even one his staunchest supporters, Sergei Kirov, argued that he had gone too far, and the plan was never executed.

Kirov

By the end of 1932, first Five Year Plan had come to an end and it was time to evaluate its success. In a report to the Politburo, Stalin described the results:

1. The results of the five-year plan have refuted the assertion of the bourgeois and Social-Democratic leaders that the five-year plan was a fantasy, delirium, an unrealizable dream. The results of the five-year plan show that the five-year plan has already been fulfilled.

2. The results of the five-year plan have shattered the well-known bourgeois "article of faith" that the working class is incapable of building the new, that it is capable only of destroying the old. The results of the five-year plan have shown that the working class is just as well able to build the new as to destroy the old.

3. The results of the five-year plan have shattered the thesis of the Social-Democrats that it is impossible to build socialism in one country taken separately. The results of the five-year plan have shown that it is quite possible to build a socialist society in one country; for the economic foundations of such a society have already been laid in the U.S.S.R.

4. The results of the five-year plan have refuted the assertion of bourgeois economists that the capitalist system of economy is the best of all systems, that every other system of economy is unstable and incapable of standing the test of the difficulties of economic development. The results of the five-year plan have shown that the capitalist system of economy is bankrupt and unstable; that it has outlived its day and must give way to another, a higher, Soviet, socialist system of economy; that the only system of economy that has no fear of crises and is able to overcome the difficulties which capitalism cannot solve, is the Soviet system of economy.

5. Finally, the results of the five-year plan have shown that the Communist Party is invincible, if it knows its goal, and if it is not afraid of difficulties.

Of course, Stalin's report failed to mention that despite his collectivization and modernization, famines across the Soviet Union resulted in the deaths of upwards of 5-10 million people. Stalin has been blamed for engineering the Ukrainian famine, to the extent that he has been accused of genocide for the mass starvation.

Chapter 15: The Great Purge

Hoping to smooth over relations between Stalin and the rest of the party, Kirov suggested in 1934 that Stalin allow those who'd been exiled for opposing him to return home. Stalin did not like this idea, and spent much of that summer trying to persuade Kirov to come back to his way of thinking. Kirov would not agree, however, and was assassinated on December 1 of that year.

Stalin claimed to know nothing of any assassination plot and insisted instead that it was the work of Trotsky and his followers. He had 17 suspects arrested, convicted and executed, including former colleagues Grigory Zinoviev and Lev Kamenev. This was just the beginning, however, and in the years that followed Stalin continued to cleanse the party of those who opposed him. With the help of Nikolai Yezhov, whom he made head of the Communist Secret Police, he saw one member after another arrested, interrogated until they confessed, and executed. By 1938, Stalin had purged so many veteran officials that he felt secure enough to stop the purges, and Yezhov became the fall guy for the excesses of the Great Purge. As a result, Yezhov was forced from his position, and his knowledge of Stalin's Great Purge made him too much of a risk to even try in public, so Yezhov was secretly executed and disposed of in 1940. After his death, Yezhov was very memorably removed from a photo showing him and Stalin, one of the most famous examples of the Soviets' historical revision.

Yezhov

Having purged the government of his enemies, Stalin turned his attention to the Soviet Army. While some historians have argued that Stalin's severe attacks on his fellow countrymen were motivated by nothing more than a paranoid need to solidify power, others maintain that he did indeed have cause for concern. Rumors definitely abounded of coups and attempted coups in the works. However, whether there was any truth behind those rumors remains a mystery.

Whatever his motivation, Stalin showed his usual thorough ruthlessness. In June of 1937 he had eight of his top commanders arrested and charged with conspiracy with Nazi Germany against the Soviet Union. The men were convicted and summarily executed. But this was just the beginning. For the next few years, the Red Army was indeed red, with the blood of 30,000 executed soldiers, including half of all the commissioned officers.

With the government and army thoroughly cleansed of opposition, Stalin attacked the Communist Secret Police. He appointed a new head, Lavrenti Beria, whom he charged with ferreting out what he called "fascist elements" that he claimed had infiltrated the police force. In reality, it was Baria's job to round up those who knew the details behind the recent killing spree and to see to it that they were silenced. In doing this, he had every leader of the police force executed.

Trotsky remained for four years in Turkey, followed by periods living in France, Norway, and finally Mexico, where he remained until his death in 1940. He continued to write at a furious pace throughout this period, composing his own history of the 1917 Revolution and a detailed analysis of what he regarded as the perversion of socialism by Stalin's bureaucracy, which he expounded on in greatest detail in his book *The Revolution Betrayed* (1936). At the same time, he organized an international movement of communists opposed to what was now called "Stalinism", a project that culminated in the creation of the Fourth International as an alternative to the Third International, the global communist organization now controlled by the Soviet state.

Trotsky reading the *Militant* in exile

Trotsky was a vocal and tireless critic of Stalin's grotesque "show trials," the humiliating convictions of Bolshevik leaders for alleged counter-revolutionary subversion. In the foreword of *The Stalin School of Falsification*, Trotsky wrote, "THE MOSCOW TRIALS, which so shocked the world, signify the death agony of Stalinism. A political regime constrained to use such methods is doomed. Depending upon external and internal circumstances, this agony may endure for a longer or shorter period of time. But no power in the world can any longer save Stalin and his system. The Soviet regime will either rid itself of the bureaucratic shell or be sucked into the abyss."

It was through this criticism that Trotsky gained his reputation as an advocate of a humane and democratic socialism. Trotsky's earlier writings about the use of Red Terror make that reputation problematic at best and disingenuous and flatly wrong at worst, but Trotskyist organizations did ultimately become an incubator of dissenting, non-doctrinaire leftist movements.

Chapter 16: Trotsky's Final Years

In 1937, Trotsky crossed the Atlantic to Mexico, where he took advantage of the welcome offered by a progressive but non-communist government. He mingled with the communist-leaning intelligentsia of Mexico City, including a stint living in the home of the painters Diego Rivera and Frida Kahlo. He also received visits from allies and sympathizers around the globe and organized with the emerging Socialist Workers' Party in the United States.

But even though he was exiled half a world away, Trotsky's days were numbered. Stalin feared his rival's growing international status, and he was never squeamish about the need for extreme methods to silence a potential enemy. Trotsky himself seemed prepared for the possibility, penning what is now called his testament in February 1940:

> "In addition to the happiness of being a fighter for the cause of socialism, fate gave me the happiness of being her husband. During the almost forty years of our life together she remained an inexhaustible source of love, magnanimity, and tenderness. She underwent great sufferings, especially in the last period of our lives. But I find some comfort in the fact that she also knew days of happiness.
>
> For forty-three years of my conscious life I have remained a revolutionist; for forty-two of them I have fought under the banner of Marxism. If I had to begin all over again I would of course try to avoid this or that mistake, but the main course of my life would remain unchanged. I shall die a proletarian revolutionist, a Marxist, a dialectical materialist, and, consequently, an irreconcilable atheist. My faith in the communist future of mankind is not less ardent, indeed it is firmer today, than it was in the days of my youth.
>
> Natasha has just come up to the window from the courtyard and opened it wider so that the air may enter more freely into my room. I can see the bright green strip of grass beneath the wall, and the clear blue sky above the wall, and sunlight everywhere. Life is beautiful. Let the future generations cleanse it of all evil, oppression and violence, and enjoy it to the full.
>
> L. Trotsky

27 February 1940

Coyoacan"

In May 1940, a cadre of Spanish and Mexican communists loyal to Stalin, including the important Mexican painter David Alfaro Siqueiros, assaulted Trotsky's home in an attempted hit. Trotsky survived, but he knew this would not be the last attempt against him. He published an account of the attempted hit, describing it vividly:

> "The attack came at dawn, about 4 A. M. I was fast asleep, having taken a sleeping drug after a hard day's work. Awakened by the rattle of gun fire but feeling very hazy, I first imagined that a national holiday was being celebrated with fireworks outside our walls. But the explosions were too close, right here within the room, next to me and overhead. The odor of gunpowder became more acrid, more penetrating. Clearly, what we had always expected was now happening: we were under attack. Where were the police stationed outside the walls? Where the guards inside? Trussed up? Kidnapped? Killed? My wife had already jumped from her bed. The shooting continued incessantly. My wife later told me that she helped me to the floor, pushing me into the space between the bed and the wall. This was quite true. She had remained hovering over me, beside the wall, as if to shield me with her body. But by means of whispers and gestures I convinced her to lie flat on the floor. The shots came from all sides, it was difficult to tell just from where. At a certain time my wife, as she later told me, was able clearly to distinguish spurts of fire from a gun: consequently, the shooting was being done right here in the room although we could not see anybody. My impression is that altogether some two hundred shots were fired, of which about one hundred fell right here, near us. Splinters of glass from windowpanes and chips from walls flew in all directions. A little later I felt that my right leg, had been slightly wounded in two places.
>
> To the uninitiated it may seem incomprehensible that Stalin's clique should have first exiled me and then should attempt to kill me abroad. Wouldn't it have been simpler to have shot me in Moscow as were so many others?
>
> The explanation is this: In 1928 when I was expelled from the party and exiled to Central Asia it was still impossible even to talk not only about shooting but arrest. The generation together with whom I went through the October revolution and the Civil War was then still alive. The political Bureau felt itself besieged from all sides. From Central Asia I was able to maintain direct contact with the opposition. In these conditions Stalin, after vacillating for one year, decided to resort to exile abroad as the lesser evil. He reasoned that Trotsky, isolated from the USSR, deprived of an apparatus and of material resources, would be powerless to undertake anything. Moreover, Stalin calculated that after he had succeeded in

completely blackening me in the eyes of the country, he could without difficulty obtain from the friendly Turkish government my return to Moscow for the final reckoning. Events have shown, however, that it is possible to participate in political life without possessing either an apparatus or material resources. With the aid of young friends I laid the foundations. of the Fourth International which is forging ahead slowly but stubbornly. The Moscow trials of 1936-1937 were staged in order to obtain my deportation from Norway, i.e., actually to hand me over into the hands of the GPU. But this did not succeed…I am informed that Stalin has several times admitted that my exile abroad was a 'major mistake.' No other way remained of rectifying the mistake except through a terrorist act."

Trotsky with supporters in 1940

Trotsky wouldn't be so lucky the second time around. On August 20, 1940, a Stalinist agent of Spanish origin named Ramón Mercader entered Trotsky's home and plunged an ice pick into his skull. Mercader later testified at his trial, "I laid my raincoat on the table in such a way as to be able to remove the ice axe which was in the pocket. I decided not to miss the wonderful opportunity that presented itself. The moment Trotsky began reading the article, he gave me my chance; I took out the ice axe from the raincoat, gripped it in my hand and, with my eyes closed, dealt him a terrible blow on the head."

Incredibly, the badly injured Trotsky was able to fight off his attacker with the help of his bodyguards, but he died the following day. His last words were allegedly, "I will not survive this attack. Stalin has finally accomplished the task he attempted unsuccessfully before."

The room where Trotsky was attacked

Chapter 17: World War II

Although Stalin was worried about internal enemies throughout the 1930s, the rest of Europe was preoccupied with the Spanish Civil War and the rise to power of Adolf Hitler and the Nazis in Germany. Seeing this as both an opportunity and a threat, Stalin threw the support of Soviet Russia behind the Popular Front supporting the Spanish Republican government in the Civil War. Not only did he send tanks and aircraft to Spain, but he also sent about 850 personnel to man them and advise the rebels in their fight.

Stalin's main concern, like that of the rest of the world at that time, was Germany. Although the Treaty of Versailles that ended the First World War had placed limits on German rearmament, those provisions were routinely being ignored by the Germans, and European powers thus sensed their own rearmament was a priority. Concerned that Hitler would soon turn his sights on Russia, he began to put out feelers among other European countries about forming an alliance. Initially, his offer was met with skepticism. English Prime Minister Neville Chamberlain disliked Stalin and would have nothing to do his offers. On the other hand, Winston Churchill, who at the time was trying to rally his countrymen to the threat posed by Hitler, saw the practical benefits of the alliance Stalin was offering, saying in a speech May 4,

1938:

"There is no means of maintaining an eastern front against Nazi aggression without the active aid of Russia. Russian interests are deeply concerned in preventing Herr Hitler's designs on Eastern Europe. It should still be possible to range all the States and peoples from the Baltic to the Black Sea in one solid front against a new outrage of invasion. Such a front, if established in good heart, and with resolute and efficient military arrangements, combined with the strength of the Western Powers, may yet confront Hitler, Goering, Himmler, Ribbentrop, Goebbels and co. with forces the German people would be reluctant to challenge."

When Chamberlain visited Hitler in September of that year, Stalin became convinced that England was planning a secret pact with Germany against the Soviet Union. Thus, he decided to try to beat them to the punch. He contacted Hitler and proposed that they form an alliance, going as far as to fire his Commissar of Foreign Affairs, Maxim Litinov, a Jew who was an unacceptable ambassador to Hitler's government. Litinov's replacement met the following month with German foreign minister Joachim von Ribbentrop and on August 28, 1939 they signed the Nazi-Soviet Pact in which both sides promised to remain neutral in any future war.

On 30 September 30 1938, Prime Minister Neville Chamberlain returned to Britain and promised the British "peace for our time", waving a copy of the agreement he had signed with Adolf Hitler and Benito Mussolini in Munich the day before. Of course, Chamberlain and Munich have become synonymous with appeasement, a word that has since taken on very negative connotations, and war would explode across the continent exactly 11 months later.

Chamberlain holds up the Munich Agreement

From 1936-1939, Hitler took a series of steps in further violation of the Treaty of Versailles, but Europe still refused to confront him. The "appeasement" of Hitler by France and Great Britain before World War II is now roundly condemned, a fact Chamberlain himself came to understand in 1939, noting, "Everything that I have worked for, everything that I have believed in during my public life, has crashed into ruins." Before World War II, however, everyone still had to deal with the haunting specter of the First World War. Thus, most British people were jubilant when Chamberlain returned from Munich in September 1938. They wanted peace, and Churchill was seen as a dangerous warmonger and imperialist who was hopelessly out of touch and out of date.

Hitler

On September 1, 1939, the world was changed forever. Despite several attempts by the French and British to appease Hitler's Nazi regime to avoid war, most notably allowing Hitler to annex the Sudetenland, Germany invaded Poland on that day, officially starting the deadliest conflict in human history. For the French and British, the Nazi invasion of Poland promised war, and by September 3 both countries declared war on Germany. Meanwhile, the Soviet Union, fresh off a nonaggression pact with Hitler, invaded the Baltic. France and the United Kingdom, treating the Soviet attack on Finland as tantamount to entering the war on the side of the Germans, responded to the Soviet invasion by supporting the USSR's expulsion from the League of Nations.

Though Germany was technically Russia's ally, Stalin had no delusions that they were friends. Instead, he used this time to build up his forces for what he saw as an inevitable invasion. First, on the heels of the German invasion of Poland in September 1939, Stalin had his troops invade and reclaim the land Russia had lost in World War I. Next he turned his attention to Finland, which was only 100 miles from the newly named Leningrad. He initially tried to negotiate with the Finnish government for some sort of treaty of mutual support. When this failed he simply invaded. While the giant Russian army ultimately won, the fact that little Finland held them off for three months demonstrated how poorly organized the bigger force was.

Britain and France also began a naval blockade of Germany on September 3 which aimed to damage the country's economy and war effort, but the Nazis would blitzkrieg across the continent over the next year and eventually overwhelm France in mid-1940, leaving the British to fight alone. For the first two years of the war, it looked as though the Axis powers may very well win the war and usher in a new world order.

Initially, Stalin believed he had several years to build up his army before Germany would invade, figuring it would at least take the Germans that long to conquer France and Britain. However, when France fell quickly in 1940, it seemed he might have miscalculated, so he again sent Molotov to Berlin to stall for time. Meanwhile, Hitler trained his sights on Britain, turning his attention to destroying the Royal Air Force as a pre-requisite for the invasion of Britain. Given how quickly the Nazis had experienced success during the war thus far, perhaps the Luftwaffe's notorious leader, Hermann Goering, was not being entirely unrealistic in 1940 when he boasted, "My Luftwaffe is invincible...And so now we turn to England. How long will this one last - two, three weeks?"

Goering

Goering, of course, was proven wrong. During the desperate air battles that ensued, Britain's investment in radar and modern fighters, coupled with a German switch in tactics, won the day. The Battle of Britain was the only battle of the war fought entirely by air, as the Luftwaffe battled the British Royal Air Force for months during the second half of 1940. The Luftwaffe also bombed British infrastructure and indiscriminately bombed civilian targets, but Germany's attempt to overwhelm the British was repulsed by the Royal Air Force. British cities were targeted, and Churchill's very public tours of wreckage helped make him an icon symbolizing the determined, stubborn resistance of the nation. This was the first real check to Nazi expansionism. In reference to the efforts of the Royal Air Force during the Battle of Britain, Churchill famously commended them, stating, "Never…was so much owed by so many to so few.". And as only Churchill could put it, "Their generals told their Prime Minister and his divided Cabinet, 'In three weeks England will have her neck wrung like a chicken.' Some chicken! Some neck!"

Stalin knew that if he could delay an invasion through the summer of 1941, he would be safe for another year. Unfortunately for Stalin, Molotov's mission failed and Hitler began to plan to invade Russia on May 15, 1941. Since military secrets are typically the hardest to keep, Stalin soon began to hear rumors of the invasion. However, when Prime Minister of England Winston Churchill contacted him in April of 1941 warning him that German troops seemed to be massing on Russia's border, Stalin remained dubious.

Stalin felt even more secure in his position when the Germans failed to invade the following May. What he did not realize was that Hitler had simply over stretched himself in Yugoslavia and only planned to delay the invasion by a few weeks. Hitler aimed to destroy Stalin's Communist regime, but he also hoped to gain access to resources in Russia, particularly oil. Throughout the first half of 1941, Germany dug in to safeguard against an Allied invasion of Western Europe as it began to mobilize millions of troops to invade the Soviet Union. Stalin even refused to believe the report of a German defector who claimed that the troops were massing on the Soviet border at that very moment.

On June 22, 1941, Stalin had to admit he was wrong; 3,400 German tanks and three million soldiers rolled across the Russian border and headed toward Leningrad, commencing Operation Barbarossa. The Soviets were so caught by surprise that the Germans were able to push several hundred miles into Russia across a front that stretched dozens of miles long, reaching the major cities of Leningrad and Sevastopol in just three months.

The first major Russian city in their path was Minsk, which fell in only six days. In order to make clear his determination to win at all costs, Stalin had the three men in charge of the troops defending Minsk executed for their failure to hold their position. This move, along with unspeakable atrocities by the German soldiers against the people of Minsk, solidified the Soviet will. In the future, Russian soldiers would fight to the death rather than surrender, and in July, Stalin exhorted the nation, "It is time to finish retreating. Not one step back! Such should now be our main slogan. ... Henceforth the solid law of discipline for each commander, Red Army soldier, and commissar should be the requirement — not a single step back without order from higher command."

Certainly their resolve was tried during the first terrible months of fighting, as Germany surrounded Leningrad and then headed toward Moscow. The worst fighting, however, was in the Ukraine. Though badly outnumbered and destined for defeat, the Soviet soldiers held off the Germans around Kiev and thus spared Moscow while it was reinforced. They suffered the worst defeat in Red Army history, but were praised as heroes by their countrymen.

In September, as winter months approached, Germany continued to advance across the countryside. This led Stalin to implement his famous "scorched earth" policy, ordering the retreating soldiers to leave nothing behind that the advancing Germans might be able to use. He also approved the formation of small bands of guerilla fighters who would remain behind the retreating army and harass the advancing German forces. These two strategies, along with Germany's ever thinning supply line, created quite a handicap for Hitler's army.

To his credit, Stalin took a page out the Royal Family of England's book and remained in Moscow even when the city was evacuated and the Germans were only fifteen miles away. He lived and worked in a bomb shelter just under the Kremlin, acting as self-appointed Supreme Commander-in-Chief and overseeing every move made by the army. He bided his time and waited until November, when the German army was forced by bad weather to end their forward movements.

The Germans had reached the vital resource centers in Russia that they were aiming for, but the sheer size of Russia had enabled the Soviet Union to mobilize millions more to fight, requiring the Germans to dig in and prepare for long term sieges, even while the notoriously harsh Russian winter was setting in.

By the summer of 1941, U.S. entry into the war seemed just on the horizon. Germany violated the Nazi-Soviet Pact and invaded the Soviet Union, spreading war to virtually every piece of the European continent. President Roosevelt and Prime Minister Winston Churchill (another powerful distant relative) met secretly off the coast of Canada in August. The two issued the Atlantic Charter, a statement of Allied goals in the war. It largely reiterated Wilsonian rights, but also specified that a US/UK victory would not lead to territorial expansion or punitive punishment.

However, a substantial segment of the American public did not appreciate the more bellicose direction President Roosevelt seemed to be heading toward. Before the "Greatest Generation" saved Western Europe, many of them were part of the largest anti-war organization in the country's history. In 1940, the United States was still mired in the Great Depression, with nearly 8,000,000 Americans still unemployed, but World War II was the most controversial issue in politics. As the Nazis raced across Western Europe in the first year of the war, young students formed the "America First Committee" in Chicago, an isolationist group supported by future presidents Gerald Ford and John F. Kennedy. The isolationist group aimed to keep the country out of European wars and focus on building America's defenses.

The group expanded to include hundreds of thousands of members by 1941, staunchly opposing President Roosevelt's "Lend-Lease" act, which helped arm the Allies. The America First Committee remained popular and powerful until the morning of December 7, 1941.

Like with Germany, the Soviet Union had signed a non-aggression pact with the Japanese, but once the Germans invaded the Soviet Union, the Japanese no longer needed to worry about their border with Russia, allowing them to focus exclusively on expanding across the Far East and various islands in the Pacific. Though the Japanese steadily expanded across the Pacific theater during 1941, they were running low on vital resources, including metal and oil. In response to Japanese aggression in China and other places, the United States had imposed a crippling embargo on Japan, exacerbating their problem. Moreover, by winter of 1941, the most obvious target for Japanese expansion was the Philippines, held by American forces.

Ironically, because both sides anticipated the potential for war in 1941, they each made key decisions that brought about the attack on Pearl Harbor. Watching Japan's expansion, the United States moved to protect the Philippines, leading President Roosevelt to station a majority of the Pacific fleet at Pearl Harbor. Japan, assuming that aggression toward British targets and the Dutch East Indies would bring the United States into the war, decided they had to inflict a blow to the United States that would set back its war effort long enough to ensure Japanese access to resources.

Japan plotted and trained for an attack on Pearl Harbor for several months leading up to December 7. Believing that a successful attack on the Pacific fleet would buy Japan enough time to win the war, the Japanese decided to focus their attack exclusively on battleships, ignoring infrastructure on the Hawaiian islands. The Japanese also knew American aircraft carriers would not be at Pearl Harbor but decided to proceed anyway.

All Americans are now familiar with the "day that will live in infamy." On December 7, 1941, the Japanese conducted a surprise attack against the naval base at Pearl Harbor (called Hawaii Operation or Operation AI by the Japanese Imperial General Headquarters). The attack was intended to keep the U.S. Pacific Fleet from interfering with Japan's military actions in Southeast Asia.

The attacks took American forces completely by surprise, inflicting massive damage to the

Pacific fleet and nearly 3,000 American casualties. Several battleships were sunk in the attack. Shortly after the attacks ended, the Japanese formally delivered a letter to the United States ending negotiations. Hours later, the Japanese invaded the Philippines, where American military leaders had anticipated a surprise attack before Pearl Harbor. Even still, the Japanese quickly overran the Philippines.

Roosevelt giving his famous speech on December 8, 1941

Roosevelt addressed Congress and the nation the following day, giving a stirring speech seeking a declaration of war against Japan. The beginning lines of the speech are instantly familiar, with Roosevelt forever marking Pearl Harbor in the national conscience as "a date which will live in infamy." Of course, the America First Committee instantly became a thing of the past, and the United States began fully mobilizing almost overnight, thanks to the peacetime draft Roosevelt had implemented. The bill helped the country's armed forces swell by two million within months of Pearl Harbor. In 1942 alone, six million men headed off to North Africa, Great Britain and the Pacific Ocean, carrying weapons in one hand and pictures of pin-up models like Betty Grable in the other. Japanese Admiral Hara Tadaichi would later comment, "We won a great tactical victory at Pearl Harbor and thereby lost the war."

The United States began 1942 determined to avenge Pearl Harbor, but the Allies, now including the Soviet Union by necessity, did not agree on the war strategy. In 1941, both the Germans and British moved armies into North Africa, where Italy had already tried and failed to reach the Suez Canal. The British sought American help in North Africa, where British General Montgomery was fighting the legendary "Desert Fox," General Erwin Rommel. At the same time, Stalin was desperate for Allied action on the European continent that could free up the pressure on the besieged Soviets. President Roosevelt had a consequential decision to make.

Roosevelt eventually decided to land American forces on North Africa to assist the British against Rommel, much to Stalin's chagrin. While the Americans and British could merely harass the Germans with air power and naval forces in the Atlantic, Stalin's Red Army had to take Hitler's best shots in Russia throughout 1942. But the Red Army's tenuous hold continued to cripple the Nazi war machine while buying the other Allies precious time.

In the dead of winter, Stalin ordered a general attack, ordering the Soviet army to throw everything it had against the Germans beginning on December 4th, 1941. The German army was caught off guard and soon driven back 200 miles. For the rest of the war, Stalin would be known for his orders to attack, attack and attack again. Because of this aggressive strategy, he was always in need of fresh troops, but it became easier to recruit willing soldiers as he demonstrated the German army was not the invincible monster everyone had feared. In fact, the Russian army's tenacity eventually became an inspiration for all the allied armies opposing Hitler.

Once the Russian winter ended, Germany once more made inroads toward Stalingrad, Stalin's own pet city. Not surprisingly, Stalin ordered that it be held no matter what. There was more than vanity at stake though. Stalingrad was all that stood between Hitler and Moscow. It also was the last major obstacle to the Russian oil fields in the Caucuses which Stalin needed and Hitler coveted. If the city fell, so would the rest of the country—and Hitler would have an invaluable resource to fuel his armies.

Stalin chose his best general, Marshal Georgy Zhukov, to lead the more than one million soldiers who would stand between Germany and the precious city. Stalin made sure that they were continually supplied with every sort of military paraphernalia available, from tanks and aircraft to guns and ammunition. He also took this opportunity to point out that his prophesy on the importance of industrialization to national security was finally proving true. Had there not been so many factories turning out weapons, the city would never have been held.

Zhukov

Zhukov, who had never been defeated, held the line until November 19, when Stalin ordered him to attack the now weary Germans. In a carefully planned pincer maneuver, the Soviet armies attacked from both the north and the south, carefully encircling the German troops until the German general, Friedrich Paulus, begged Hitler to allow him to withdraw. But by then the Fuhrer was obsessed with capturing the city that he refused his general's pleas, so the Germans attempted to hold on, losing thousands of additional men without taking the city. When Paulus surrendered on January 30, he had lost 1.5 million men and over 6,000 tanks and aircraft.

Entering 1943, the Allies looked to press their advantage in the Pacific and Western Europe. The United States was firmly pushing the Japanese back across the Pacific, while the Americans and British plotted a major invasion somewhere in Western Europe to relieve the pressure on the Soviets, who had just lifted the siege of Stalingrad. The Allies were now firmly winning the war. From January 14th to the 24th of 1943, Roosevelt, Churchill and other Allied leaders met in Casablanca, Morocco, but Stalin declined so that he could stay back and manage affairs in Stalingrad. The Casablanca Conference set out Allies demands for an unconditional surrender of Axis Powers. The leaders also agreed to the first major allied assault on Europe: an invasion from North Africa via Sicily into Germany. Roosevelt also agreed to increase submarine bombing in the Atlantic and to send more aid to the Soviet Union

Even before the British and Americans were able to make major strategic decisions in 1943, the massive German surrender at Stalingrad marked the beginning of the end for Hitler's armies in Russia. From that point forward, the Red Army started to steadily push the Nazis backward toward Germany. Yet it would still take the Red Army almost an entire two years to push the Germans all the way out of Russia. In July, just a few months after the surrender at Stalingrad, the Allies conducted what at the time was the largest amphibious invasion in history, coordinating the landing of two whole armies on Sicily, over a front more than 100 miles long. Within weeks of the beginning of the Allied campaign in Italy, Italy's government wasted no time negotiating peace with the Allies and quickly quit the war.

Though Italy was no longer fighting for the Axis, German forces continued to occupy and control Italy in 1943. The Germans attempted to resist the Allies' invasion on Sicily but were badly outmanned and outgunned, leading to a German evacuation of the island within a month. The Allies would land on the mainland of Italy in September and continue to campaign against the Germans there.

Stalingrad proved to be Germany's high water-mark against the Soviet Union. For the rest of the war, they were in a constant state of retreat. As the Red Army chased them out and retook more and more of the countryside, they were appalled by the treatment both soldiers and civilians had received at the German's hands. Over four million Soviet prisoners of war had died of starvation, sickness and other forms of mistreatment. In continuation of the "Final Solution," they had also killed all the Jews they captured, as well as civilians of any other ethnic group Hitler didn't care for. It seems that their thought process was that the more Soviet people they killed, the fewer they'd have to deal with later. It has been estimated that the invading Nazis completely razed over 10,000 Russian villages to the ground, slaughtering all the inhabitants they could get their hands on.

As word of German genocide spread throughout the Soviet Union it had a galvanizing rather than weakening effect. Instead of surrendering to the invading forces in hopes of receiving fair treatment, the Soviet peasants would hide in the woods when they heard of an approaching German army. From there, they would organize guerrilla groups that would strike at the Germans from all angles, picking off sentries, disrupting supply lines and spreading chaos.

Likewise, the Russian soldier knew that he had a better chance of survival in the field of battle than if they were taken prisoner, so they were more than willing to fight to the death.

Following the victory at Stalingrad, Stalin was gratified to be invited to join Churchill and Franklin Delano Roosevelt at a secret conference in Teheran in November 1943. Once ostracized by the now disgraced Chamberlain, Stalin must have felt vindicated as he sat down as a member of "The Big Three." However, his pleasure was short lived as Churchill and Roosevelt once more denied his request that the allies immediately open up a second front to drive the Germans out of Western Europe. Unfortunately Stalin's own success at Stalingrad had demonstrated that England and the United States were not as necessary to Soviet survival as Stalin had once claimed.

Of course, Stalin was no fool; he knew that these men trusted him no more than he trusted them. However, while his conclusion was correct (Britain and America disliked the Soviet system and would have loved to have seen it fall,) his concerns that they would someday sign a peace treaty with Hitler were completely unfounded.

In his defense, Stalin was at a disadvantage. He was something like the out of town stranger that someone had brought home for Thanksgiving Dinner. England and America were related both ethnically and politically. They also spoke the same language, ate the same sorts of foods and shared a mutual history going back nearly 1,000 years. Russia, on the other hand, was a mystery, a separate entity steeped in archaic tradition and mystery. Therefore, Stalin could not help but feel like an outsider.

Still, Stalin had no problem holding his own when it came time to talk of military strategy. Lord Alan Brooke, a British Field Marshall and Churchill's aid, kept a lengthy diary of the conference. This is how he described Stalin:

> "During this meeting and all the subsequent ones which we had with Stalin, I rapidly grew to appreciate the fact that he had a military brain of the very highest calibre. Never once in any of his statements did he make any strategic error, nor did he ever fail to appreciate all the implications of a situation with a quick and unerring eye. In this respect he stood out compared with his two colleagues."

Ultimately, Stalin sided with Roosevelt and pressured the British into accepting a cross-channel invasion of France for the following year. Churchill was reluctantly forced to recognize that Britain had become the junior partner in the enterprise.

Churchill disagreed with the planning of Operation Overlord, but he lost his argument. Though the Allies used misinformation to try deceiving the Germans, all sides understood that the most sensible place for an invasion logistically was across the English Channel. The Germans had constructed the Atlantic Wall, a network of coastal fortifications throughout France, to defend against just this kind of invasion. Thus, the Allies devised an extremely complex amphibious attack that would be precipitated by naval and air bombardment, paratroopers, and even inflatable tanks that would be able to fire on fortifications from the coastline, all while landing nearly 150,000 men across nearly 70 miles of French beaches. The Allies would then use their beachhead to create an artificial dock, eventually planning to land nearly 1 million men in France.

During the first half of 1944, the Americans and British began a massive buildup of men and resources in the United Kingdom, while Eisenhower and the military leaders devised an enormous and complex amphibious invasion of Western Europe. Though the Allies theoretically had several different staging grounds for an attack on different sides of the continent, the most obvious place for an invasion was just across the English Channel from Britain into France. And though the Allies used misinformation to deceive the Germans, Hitler's men built an extensive network of coastal fortifications throughout France to protect against just such an invasion.

Largely under the supervision of Rommel, the Germans constructed the "Atlantic Wall", across which reinforced concrete pillboxes for German defenders were built close to the beaches for infantry to use machine guns and anti-tank artillery. Large obstacles were placed along the beaches to effectively block tanks on the ground, while mines and underwater obstacles were planted to stop landing craft from getting close enough.

Atlantic Wall 1942-1944

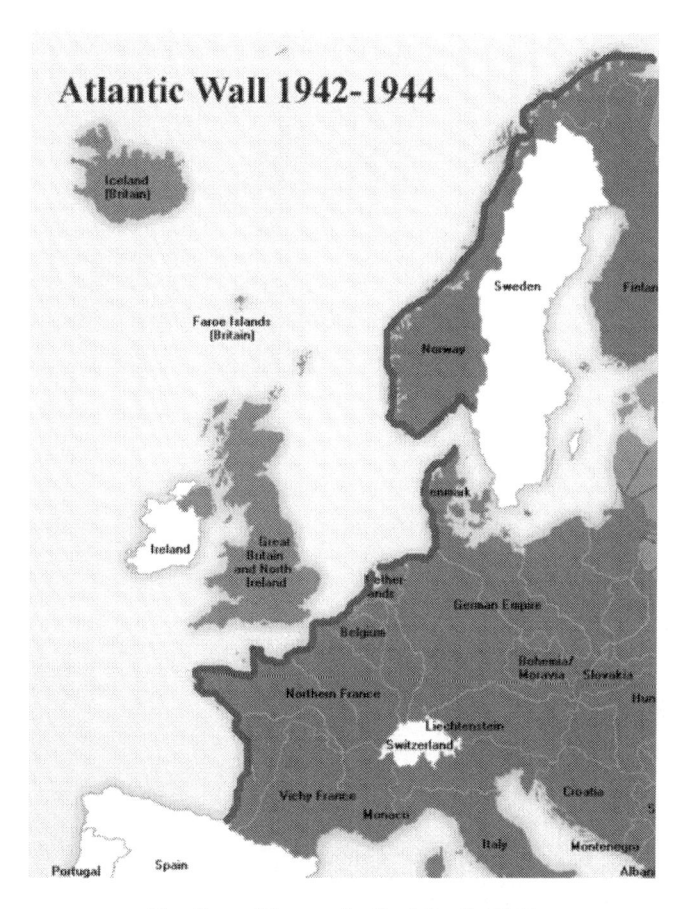

The Green Line marks the Atlantic Wall

Throughout the first half of 1944, France, once a lightly defended area used largely for the recuperation of German soldiers from the Eastern front, was now the focus of Allied and German attention, with feverish plans made for the region on both sides. Reinforcements flooded into Northern France while tacticians planned for the impending invasion and counter-attack. The speed with which Germany had reinforced and strengthened the region meant that the Allies were less than certain of the success of the invasion. Britain, weary of amphibious landings after the disastrous Expeditionary Force campaign of 1940 came perilously close complete obliteration, was more than anxious. Allied military fortunes had been, at best, mixed. Professor Newton points out Britain, together with its continental allies, had lost its foothold in Europe but had managed to bloody the nose of Germany in the Battle of Britain in the summer of 1940. The

Allies had lost Crete, yet stopped the Afrika Corps at El Alamein. With its American allies, Britain had successfully invaded Italy before becoming entangled in the costly German defense of the country. Britain, as a small island nation, lacked the manpower and supplies needed to singlehandedly defeat the German military. In comparison, the United States, an industrial colossus, had ample men and materials. Like Britain, American fortunes in the European theater were mixed, ranging from the successful landings in North Africa to the debacle of Kasserine Pass.

Storming Omaha Beach

Churchill was not overstating the achievements of *Operation Overlord* when he described the plan "the greatest thing we have ever attempted". On D-Day, the greatest armada the world had ever seen had landed 170,000 soldiers on the heavily defended beaches of Normandy in just 24 hours. More remarkable was the fact that the operation was a success on every major level. Deception, tactical surprise and overwhelming force had contributed to the establishment of an adequate beachhead. Confusion and dissent had stopped the Germans massing for any great counterattack. The Atlantic Wall which Hitler had placed so much faith in had been breached, and the race to Paris was on.

Operation Overlord aimed to have the Allies reach the Seine River within 3 months of D-Day, and it's a testament to the men who fought and served on D-Day that the goal was reached early. To do so, the Allies overcame firm resistance from the Germans, atrocious weather that limited resupply for the Allies, and the difficult terrain of Normandy, which included endless hedgerows providing hidden cover. And the Allies reached their objective ahead of time despite the fact the objectives of D-Day were not entirely met; the Allies had not captured Caen, St-lo or Bayeux on the first day.

Nevertheless, the landings were clearly a resounding success. Casualties were significantly smaller than those expected by commanders, and the significance of D-Day to the morale of the Western world, much of it under German domination, cannot be underestimated. For France, Poland, Czechoslovakia, Belgium, Holland and more, who had suffered over four years of occupation, the great democracies were finally coming to their rescue. American, British, Canadian, Polish, Commonwealth, Greek, Belgian, Dutch and Norwegian soldiers, sailors, and airmen all participated in the Battle for Normandy, which saw the Allies on the banks of the Seine River just 80 days after D-Day.

Sensing victory, the Allies began planning for a post-war world in the months after D-Day. In July 1944, diplomats from 44 nations come together in Bretton Woods, New Hampshire, where they established the International Monetary Fund (IMF). Otherwise known as the World Bank, the organization was aimed at providing funds for reconstructing countries devastated by war. The following month, the U.S., Great Britain, China and the USSR met at the Dumbarton Oaks Conference to begin planning the formation of a stronger League of Nations, this time to be called the United Nations.

After D-Day had all but sealed the Allied victory, Stalin's Red Army became more aggressive in retaking land formerly held by Germany. Concerned over the ever widening Soviet map, Churchill met with Stalin in October of 1944 (Roosevelt was by this time too frail to join them) and, while ceding Rumania and Bulgaria to the Soviets, insisted that Yugoslavia and Hungary be shared among the allies.

The sticking point, however, was Poland. Stalin demanded that the very anti-communist Polish government in exile be overturned in favor of a one more sympathetic to his regime. Churchill, on the other hand, felt a sense of obligation to the government as it stood, since they were hiding out in London. However, he wisely agreed to table the subject until the end of the war was clearly in sight.

In October 1944 Churchill met Stalin in a bilateral meeting in Moscow. He purported to divide the post war European states up proportionately, in terms of British and Soviet influence.

Bulgaria would be 75% Soviet, for example. Stalin appeared to agree, but this was naive nonsense. Not only did it ignore Britain's diminishing role, but it was hard to envision how democratic Britain could share influence with an expansionist Soviet dictatorship within one given state. This scheme would ultimately be vetoed by the Americans, in an episode which further undermined Churchill's relationship with Roosevelt. Yet Stalin's apparent "acceptance" of Britain's suppression of the Greek communists in December 1944, seemed to accord with the deal and certainly led Churchill to trust him more than he should have done when they met with Roosevelt at Yalta.

The three leaders at Yalta

When The Big Three met once again, this time at Yalta, Stalin's home turf, the Allies were pressing down upon Germany from both the east and the west, and with the war in Europe in its final months and nearing an end, the meeting was intended mainly to discuss the re-establishment of the nations of war-torn Europe. Within a few years, with the Cold War dividing the continent, Yalta became a subject of intense controversy. To some extent, it has remained controversial. Among the agreements, the Conference called for Germany's unconditional surrender, the split of Berlin, German demilitarization and reparations, the status of Poland, and Russian involvement in the United Nations

By this time Stalin had thoroughly established Soviet authority in most of Eastern Europe and made it clear that he had no intention of giving up lands his soldiers had fought and died for. The best he would offer Churchill and Roosevelt was the promise that he would allow free elections to be held. He made it clear, though, that the only acceptable outcome to any Polish election would be one that supported communism. One Allied negotiator would later describe Stalin's very formidable negotiating skills. "Marshal Stalin as a negotiator was the toughest proposition of all. Indeed, after something like thirty years' experience of international conferences of one kind and another, if I had to pick a team for going into a conference room, Stalin would be my first choice. Of course the man was ruthless and of course he knew his purpose. He never wasted a word. He never stormed, he was seldom even irritated."

The final question lay in what to do with a conquered Germany. Both the Western Allies and Stalin wanted Berlin, and knew that whoever held the most of it when the truce was signed would end up controlling the city. Thus they spent the next several months pushing their generals further and further toward this goal, but the Russians got there first. Thus, when the victorious allies met in Potsdam in 1945, it remained Britain and America's task to convince Stalin to divide the country, and even the city, between them. They accomplished this, but at a terrible cost: Russia got liberated Austria.

At the same time, there was a sense of political change in the air. President Roosevelt had died and been replaced by the more down to earth and boisterous Harry Truman in April 1945. Also, while the conference was in session, the British elected the Labour Party into power, replacing Churchill with a new and untried Prime Minister, Clement Attlee. It is little wonder, then, that Stalin was able to gain such concessions, since he was the only one there who had been through the entire process.

Though the countries had often discussed Russia joining America and Britain's fight against the Japanese, it became clear at Potsdam that this was not going to happen. Instead, Stalin pleaded for help for his own country, which had been decimated by the fighting with Germany. Russia had lost more than 30,000 factories and so much farm land that the vast majority of the population was suffering from malnutrition. However, he failed to get much of a sympathetic hearing from Truman who, unlike his predecessor, was not particularly interested in the global picture.

Stalin was, however, and he was particularly concerned that the Allies might stage an invasion of Russia and overthrow his regime. While it may have seemed at the time that he was just being paranoid, we now know that George Patton was already pushing Truman and the other world leaders to go ahead and finish the weakened Soviets off. Thus, Stalin was actually wise to build up Communist governments in Czechoslovakia, East Germany, Bulgaria and elsewhere.

The British and Americans didn't see it that way, though. Instead, they assumed that Stalin was expanding the Soviet Union in preparation for invading Europe. The Europeans appealed to the Americans for help and with them created the North Atlantic Treaty Organization in 1949. This mutual mistrust among all parties involved marked the beginning of the Cold War.

World War II was so horrific that in its aftermath, the victorious Allies sought to address every aspect of it to both punish war criminals and attempt to ensure that there was never a conflict like it again. World War II was unprecedented in terms of the global scale of the fighting, the number of both civilian and military casualties, the practice of total war, and war crimes. World War II also left two undisputed, ideologically opposed superpowers standing, shaping global politics over the last 65 years. As a result, World War II's legacies are still strongly felt today. In the wake of the war, the European continent was devastated, leaving the Soviet Union and the United States as uncontested superpowers. This ushered in over 45 years of the Cold War, and a political alignment of Western democracies against the Communist Soviet bloc that literally split Berlin in two.

Chapter 18: The Cold War

At the end of World War II, Stalin hoped to continue to expand Soviet influence by blockading West Berlin, which was occupied by France, the United Kingdom and the United States. After the war, Germany had been split up into four parts, one part for each of the four major Allies, and though Berlin was in the Soviet Union's sector, it was also split four ways. The Western allies therefore had an enclave in West Berlin that was totally surrounded by communist territory, and Stalin then ordered a blockade of all supplies into West Berlin, hoping the other Allies would cede the city to the Soviet sector of Germany.

However, the United States and its allies were able to organize a massive airlift of supplies that kept the city of West Berlin supplied. Over the next 11 months, between June 1948 and May 1949 England, America and several other western European countries delivered thousands of tons of food and fuel to the city. The Soviet Union and its German allies eventually stopped the blockade when they realized the West could continue to supply Berlin by air indefinitely. As a result of their heroic efforts, West Berlin survived and Stalin was beaten.

Stalin's next great mistake involved Korea. Korea had been occupied by Japan and was ceded to the Allies after World War II. Without taking into consideration the fact that he had ordered his Soviet representative to the United Nations to withdraw, he persuaded North Korean dictator Kim il-Sung to invade South Korea. In 1950, communist Korean forces, with communist Chinese and Soviet support, invaded South Korea, which was supported by the West. The communist forces hoped to occupy all of Korea and make it a communist state

When the U.N. voted to send troops to oppose the spread of communism, there was not a Soviet representative present to exercise the country's veto power in the Security Council. The resulting war lasted over three years, and saw the United States military fighting communist forces in battle for the first time. The western forces almost captured the entire Korean peninsula until the communist Chinese entered the war. After much fighting, the two sides agreed on a cease-fire line at the original border at the 38th parallel. The cease-fire line created the border between western ally South Korea and communist North Korea.

Although the Russians were indirectly involved in the Korean War, the important result of the Korean War was that the Red Scare spread like wild fire through the United States, deteriorating U.S.-Soviet relations to an all-time low. In the decade that followed, it would become clear to the world that power was no longer divided among many little countries in the world but instead rested almost exclusively in the hands of the U.S. and the USSR. The Korean War was also the first example of America's containment strategy, which sought to protect non-communist nations from communist aggression to prevent the spread of communism to other countries. Containment would remain the primary American foreign policy strategy for decades.

When World War II was over, the United States and Soviet Union turned their attention from Nazi Germany to each other. Both sides began secretly working to recruit the Nazi scientists involved with designing the V-2 rockets and bring them to Russia and America, in effect giving them immunity from prosecution for war crimes. One of these Nazi scientists, Wernher von Braun, was instrumental in the development of V-2 rockets for the Nazis, and he was brought to America by the Truman Administration. Von Braun became more important than any American in the development of American rockets. In the 1950s he helped design the Jupiter class of rockets. When the United States fell behind the Soviets in the Space Race, they relied more heavily on von Braun's designs. When Apollo 11 lifted off into space, it was riding atop a Saturn V rocket designed by von Braun.

Von Braun

With the end of the war, American and Soviet scientists gained access to the plans and specifications of the German V-2 rocket. The two sides now had their hands on important, sensitive research, made all the more necessary due to the fact that their technology was well behind the Nazis' at the end of the war.

Even before the war, American scientists were experimenting with rocketry. Unlike the Germans, however, the Americans were unable to create a rocket that propelled into outer space. Regardless, the nation's scientists were actually the first to create a liquid-fueled rocket in Auburn, Massachusetts, in 1926. Four years later, the American Interplanetary Society was created in New York City, to promote the study of space travel.

Throughout the war, however, neither the Americans nor the Soviets were able to match the power of German ingenuity when it came to space exploration. With the war's end, the Americans and the Soviets seized the V-2 rocket components and specifications, sending them home to their respective laboratories for additional study. The United States harnessed the intellectual might of nearly 700 German scientists through Truman's top secret "Operation Paperclip", which stealthily relocated the scientists into America.

While the U.S. successfully brought in Nazi scientists, the proximity of Germany to Russia helped ensure it would be the Soviet Union that took much of the Nazi infrastructure left behind. Because the Soviets occupied East Germany, where much of the V-2 program was developed, it was able to capture and utilize the rocketry facilities. Quietly, the two nations began a race into space, using German advances as a springboard.

With these German resources in hand, both the Americans and the Soviets were able to project their own rockets into outer space within just a few years. Although Sputnik 1 will forever be celebrated as the first satellite to orbit Earth, America beat the Soviets in the race to project *something* into space. On March 22nd, 1946, the United States became the second nation in the world to propel an object into outer space when it successfully launched an exact replica of a German V-2 rocket outside of the earth's atmosphere. Later that year, the U.S. attached a motion picture camera to a V-2 and was able to take the first photographs and videos of the Earth from outer space. In 1947, the U.S. made great advances in using rocketry to transport living beings into space when in launched fruit flies into space aboard a V-2 rocket. Though they were just flies, this marked the first time a living organism travelled outside the earth's atmosphere.

Across the world, the Soviets were not so quick to enter space. The U.S. had the benefit not only of German scientists, but also of having German V-2 rockets on hand. It was thus much easier to copy the V-2 in America than in the Soviet Union, which only had specifications, blueprints and building materials. During the rest of the 1940s, the Soviets were playing catch-up on a variety of fronts, including the space and arms races. While the U.S. had detonated a nuclear bomb in 1945, the Soviets were not able to achieve that milestone until 1949, and while the U.S. now had a workable ballistic missile in the V-2, the Soviets would not have their own until the mid-1950s. Across the Soviet sphere, there was an intellectual disdain for space travel, which was considered impractical and irrelevant to the aims of the country, but space technology was vital for reaching military superiority or at least military equality with America.

When Stalin was first informed by the other Allied leaders about the existence of a new secret weapon, the atomic bomb, he had to feign surprise and ignorance about it. In fact, Stalin's regime had been working on a nuclear weapons program since 1942, relying greatly upon successful Soviet espionage to help lead the way. With intelligence sources connected to the Manhattan Project, Stalin was able to keep abreast of the Allies' progress toward creating an atomic bomb. By 1945, the Soviets already had a working blueprint of America's first atomic bombs.

On August 29, 1949, the Soviets successfully tested an atomic bomb, and with that, the Soviet Union became the second nation after the U.S. to develop and possess nuclear weapons.

The first Soviet test of an atomic weapon

In early 1951, the United States established "Project MX-1593", a top secret and heavily funded program that became part of the U.S. Air Force. The purpose of MX-1593 was to create an intercontinental ballistic missile capable of carrying a nuclear warhead. The aim was, obviously, to establish a system allowing the U.S. to target a Soviet site anywhere in the world remotely.

With Project MX-1593, America seemed to hold the advantage in creating an ICBM, and von Braun had been part of the Nazi team that envisioned rockets that could bomb the East Coast of the United States itself, which would have required an intercontinental ballistic missile (ICBM). However, the Germans were unable to achieve this goal. Since von Braun had already begun the research for an ICBM, the Americans seemed positioned to make enormous progress.

However, it was the Soviets who were first to create an ICBM. On August 21st, 1957, the Soviets launched the R-7 Semyorka, which was the world's first intercontinental ballistic missile. Work on the project began in 1953, while the American program had begun two years prior, but the Soviets were nonetheless able to complete the mission earlier. The first successful test launch in 1957 allowed the missile to travel nearly 4,000 miles.

Soviet eagerness to develop an ICBM was fueled in part by the superiority of the U.S. Air Force, which was larger and more advanced than the Soviet arsenal. Thus, the USSR felt it needed alternative ways to deliver nuclear warheads into American territory if its nuclear arsenal were to remain strategically relevant and military equity or superiority was to be achieved. The creation of the ICBM essentially negated the superiority of the U.S. Air Force, erasing all strategic edges the U.S. held over the USSR. At the same time, with this success, the Soviets opened nearly a decade of dominance of space exploration, which culminated in the launching of the world's first human being into outer space.

Chapter 19: Stalin's Death

Among the major differences between the two superpowers was their leadership. While America gained a new and fresh president every 4-8 years, Russia had been under Stalin's control for over two decades. As his health began to fail, it became apparent that he had no intention of stepping down or even looking around for a worthy successor. In fact, those who were even whispered to be interested in his position often met with bad ends. Thus, when a rumor began to go around about a plot against his life, his closest associates panicked and began to make plans to leave the country.

Around the end of 1952 and the beginning of 1953, it seemed Stalin was on the verge of conducting another purge, starting by falsifying the "Doctors' Plot", which was to accuse Jewish doctors of plotting to assassinate top Communist leaders. In addition to being obviously anti-Semitic, it has long been assumed that Stalin was going to use it as a pretext to actually purge party leaders.

As it turned out, Stalin didn't have enough time to conduct the plan. He had suffered a major heart attack in 1945 and was suffering from various other maladies by the time he had reached his mid-70s. On March 1, 1945, Stalin did not come out of his bedroom, alarming authorities who finally entered his room that night to find him lying on the floor, seemingly having suffered a stroke. When he died the next morning, the official cause of death was listed as a cerebral hemorrhage.

Since Stalin's death in early March 1953, there have been a number of conspiracy theories suggesting that he was actually murdered. Ex-Communists and other political enemies have since claimed that Stalin was poisoned by Lavrentiy Beria, who allegedly boasted that he poisoned Stalin to prevent the coming purge. Nikita Khrushchev would later recall that Beria seemed ecstatic upon finding Stalin near death on the night of March 1, even while other party leaders were too fearful to take action based on the possibility Stalin would recover and take vengeance on them. Decades later, some historians continue to speculate that Stalin was poisoned by warfarin, a powerful rat poison that causes the kind of hemorrhagic stroke he suffered.

Chapter 20: Lenin's Legacy

Though he was a political genius, Lenin had made more than his fair share of enemies, even among his own party, through the years. And during the months leading up to his death, they were already beginning to jockey for position. Thus, by the time he was gone, several of them had plans for the government that they planned to put in place. The most significant among these was to move the country from a more socialist style of government to one dominated by communism and government ownership of business and farms.

Though Stalin had been a loyal follower of Lenin's for years, Lenin still felt that he was not the right successor to head the Soviet government. Instead, he recommended the post be given to Leon Trotsky. However, Stalin got wind of this plan and positioned himself and his followers to take control of the government as soon as Lenin was pronounced dead. While Lenin had been severe, Stalin was positively bloodthirsty. His cruel tactics would terrorize the entire Soviet Union and much of the world for the next several decades.

It must also be remembered that everyone in Lenin's inner circle were themselves rebels on one level or another. They did not overthrow the Tsar out of loyalty to the government, nor were they inclined to compromise on policies that they disagreed with. Thus, having "lived by the sword," of revolution, the Bolsheviks would ultimately "die by the sword" of their own personalities.

Lenin will forever be remembered as the foremost Soviet revolutionary and the founder of the Soviet Union, but his voluminous writings continue to be read by socialists and historians alike. As one biographer put it, his works "reveal in detail a man with iron will, self-enslaving self-discipline, scorn for opponents and obstacles, the cold determination of a zealot, the drive of a fanatic, and the ability to convince or browbeat weaker persons by his singleness of purpose, imposing intensity, impersonal approach, personal sacrifice, political astuteness, and complete conviction of the possession of the absolute truth." Put simply, Lenin's life "became the history of the Bolshevik movement."

The unrelenting passion and drive was picked up on by those who met Lenin, including British historian Bertrand Russell, who wrote, "He is very friendly, and apparently simple, entirely without a trace of hauteur. If one met him without knowing who he was, one would not guess that he is possessed of great power or even that he is in any way eminent. I have never met a personage so destitute of self-importance. He looks at his visitors very closely, and screws up one eye, which seems to increase alarmingly the penetrating power of the other. He laughs a great deal; at first his laugh seems merely friendly and jolly, but gradually I came to feel it rather grim. He is dictatorial, calm, incapable of fear, extraordinarily devoid of self-seeking, an embodied theory. The materialist conception of history, one feels, is his life-blood. He resembles a professor in his desire to have the theory understood and in his fury with those who misunderstand or disagree, as also in his love of expounding, I got the impression that he despises a great many people and is an intellectual aristocrat."

For better or worse, Lenin was the philosophical driving force and a real-life inspiration for revolutionaries across the globe. In addition to fueling the Soviet Union, which officially rendered him infallible while it was in operation, Lenin had an effect on successful revolutions across the globe, including those of Fidel Castro, Mao Zedong, and Ho Chi Minh. Naturally, this has been both celebrated and condemned.

Perhaps the dueling narratives were most poignantly juxtaposed upon his death. Upon hearing the news, Chinese premier Sun Yat-sen glowingly stated, "Through the ages of world history, thousands of leaders and scholars appeared who spoke eloquent words, but these remained words. You, Lenin, were an exception. You not only spoke and taught us, but translated your words into deeds. You created a new country. You showed us the road of joint struggle... You, great man that you are, will live on in the memories of the oppressed people through the centuries."

Giving voice to the other side of the argument was none other than the British Bulldog, who aptly summed up Lenin's life and legacy better than perhaps anyone since. An opponent of the Bolshevik Revolution and a supporter of the Whites during the Russian Civil War, Winston Churchill claimed, "He alone could have found the way back to the causeway... The Russian people were left floundering in the bog. Their worst misfortune was his birth... their next worst his death."

Chapter 21: Stalin's Legacy

When Joseph Stalin died in early March of 1953, his death was greeted with more relief than sadness and more joy than grief. In 1956, Stalin's successor, Nikita Khrushchev, openly repudiated Stalin's political policies before a Congress of Communist Party leaders, declaring Stalin's reign a "violation of Leninist norms of legality". Khrushchev subsequently freed most of those whom Stalin had imprisoned, including thousands of otherwise loyal party members.

Over time, more and more was done to try to eradicate the memory of Stalin in Russia. The government pulled down statues, renamed streets and even changed the name of his beloved Stalingrad to Volgograd. The only thing they forgot was that, like Hitler, Stalin had a lot of support from his fellow countrymen during his life. While he had the blood of millions on his hands, it is doubtful that anyone in his party could dare to call their hands clean.

This monument to Stalin in Gori was destroyed in 2010

Still, the Soviets were more than content to place all the blame for the Stalinist era's excesses at the leader's feet. One Soviet book summed up the prevailing view of Stalin in the wake of his death:

> J. V. Stalin had held, since 1922, the post of General Secretary of the Communist Party Central Committee. He had made important contributions to the implementation of the Party's policy of socialist construction in the USSR, and he had won great popularity by his relentless fight against the anti-Leninist groups of the Trotskyites and Bukharinites. Since the early 1930s, however, all the successes achieved by the Soviet people in the building of socialism began to be arbitrarily attributed to Stalin. Already in a letter written back in 1922 Lenin warned the Party Central Committee: "Comrade Stalin," he wrote, "having become General Secretary, has concentrated boundless authority in his hands, and I am not sure whether he will always be able to exercise that authority with sufficient discretion." During the first few years after Lenin's death Stalin reckoned with his critical remarks. As time passed, however, he abused his position of General Secretary of the Party Central Committee more and more

frequently, violating the principle of collective leadership and making independent decisions on important Party and state issues. Those personal shortcomings of which Lenin had warned manifested themselves with greater and greater insistence: his rudeness, capriciousness, intolerance of criticism, arbitrariness, excessive suspiciousness, etc. This led to unjustified restrictions of democracy, gross violations of socialist legality and repressions against prominent Party, government and military leaders and other people.

Chapter 22: Trotsky's Legacy

Since he only wielded power for a short time, it is hard to know what a Trotsky-led Soviet Union would have looked like and how greatly it would have differed from the country that Stalin created. However, no matter how later admirers and observers have essentially attempted to whitewash Trotsky's legacy, it's safe to assume that a Soviet Union led by Trotsky instead of Stalin would have differed in degree but not kind. When in power, Trotsky was never opposed to the use of violence, coercion, and repression of dissent, even if he never implemented anything close to the scale of Stalin's terror.

Regardless of his leadership, Trotsky's lasting legacy has been his voluminous writings, which were both theoretical and historical. He had a profound influence as an early and forceful critic of the direction of Soviet rule under Stalin, to the extent that his works were banned in the Soviet Union until the late 1980s. Trotsky was also a crucial analyst of the nature of totalitarian bureaucracy as a new 20th century mode of oppression, and his status as a symbol of the far left has had an important if eccentric role in many modern political and cultural debates.

Trotsky's itinerant life also unites a number of the disparate nodal points of 20th century culture and intellectual life. He spent his school years in the cosmopolitan port of Odessa that was later memorialized in the stories of Soviet Russia's great Jewish writer, Isaac Babel. Prior to the first Russian Revolution of 1905, Trotsky lived in London, the same city teeming with exiles and international political intrigue where Karl Marx himself had spent most of his later life. Later, in the years before the First World War he lived in Vienna and frequented the Café Central, whose other regulars included Sigmund Freud, Theodore Herzl, the Logical Positivist philosophers, and Adolf Hitler. The eve of the Russian Revolution of 1917 found Trotsky living in New York City, writing for radical newspapers in the company of fellow Russian Nikolai Bukharin, who would later be a Bolshevik ally and rival. Trotsky's final exile was spent in post-revolutionary Coyoacán, a neighborhood of Mexico City also home to Diego Rivera and Frida Kahlo, with whom he stayed on his initial arrival to Mexico. Prior to Stalinist agent Ramón Mercader's successful assassination, Trotsky narrowly escaped being murdered by none other than David Alfaro Siqueiros, Rivera a great painter and muralist like Rivera but also a fervent supporter of Stalin. Trotsky thus ends up resembling a kind of Zelig figure, present in many of the major locations of modern cultural and intellectual life.

It is not clear what legacy Trotsky will have in a post-communist world as the representative of a relatively obscure strain of what has now become a relatively marginal ideology. The conflicts that defined his life and ultimately led to his brutal death have been replaced by other conflicts mapped onto very different geographies. While opposition to capitalism persists in many forms, it does not tend to draw much from the once-paradigmatic Russian revolutionaries of 1917, who shocked the world when they swept into power in one of the most politically reactionary and culturally traditional countries in Europe. Trotsky's political and intellectual life emerged out of what was at the time the unprecedented effort to put the theories of Marx and Engels into practice in an environment that did not seem particularly ripe to become the vanguard of world politics. The effort to make sense of Trotsky's political career and legacy thus provides an invaluable window into the driving conflicts of what may seem like the increasingly distant world of the early 20th century.

Stalin caused Trotsky's name to be erased from official histories of the Russian Revolution and the Bolshevik party, and it was not until 2001 that Trotsky was officially "rehabilitated" by the Russian government as an important historical figure and a major intellectual. Trotsky's legacy in the 20th century resembled his own life in his final years; his followers were marginal and powerless, but also passionate and tireless in pursuing their own vision against the odds. There has been much speculation as to how Soviet history would have differed had Trotsky, rather than Stalin, succeeded Lenin. All in all, it seems unlikely based on his exercise of power that Trotsky would have ruled in a particularly humane manner if he had remained anything like the fierce and ruthless Trotsky who led the Red Army to victory in the years after the revolution. It seems even unlikelier if he remained the Trotsky who wrote *Terrorism and Communism*. His denunciations of Stalinist totalitarianism seem to have been a tactical ideological shift that was successful in creating a sympathetic reputation for himself.

It is probably a stretch to say that the humiliating experience of political failure and exile humanized Trotsky and led him to sympathize with others consigned to the "dustbin of history", given how he had treated them when he exercised nearly unrivaled power. But debates over his life, work, and legacy continue, and it is those questions that make Trotsky an intriguing and relative figure today, more than 20 years after the collapse of the revolution he helped lead.

Bibliography

Trotsky and Lenin were tireless writers who wrote dozens of articles, books, pamphlets, and more. A large collection of their works have been archived at http://www.marxists.org/archive/trotsky/works/index.htm#a1901

Brouè Pierre, *Trotsky*, ed. Fayard, Paris, 1988

Cliff, Tony (1989–93) *Trotsky* (4 Vols.) London: Bookmarks

Deutscher, Isaac *Trotsky: The Prophet Armed (1954)*

Trotsky: The Prophet Unarmed (1959)

Trotsky: The Prophet Outcast (1963)

Daniels, Robert V (1991) *Trotsky, Stalin & Socialism.*

Dunn, Bill & Radice, Hugo eds. *Permanent Revolution – Results and Prospects 100 Years On*

Dimitri Volkogonov (1996) *Trotsky, the Eternal Revolutionary.*

Gilbert, Helen (2003) *Leon Trotsky: His Life and Ideas.*

Hallas, Duncan (1979) *Trotsky's Marxism*

Hansen, Joseph, ed. (1969) *Leon Trotsky: the Man and His Work. Reminiscences and Appraisals.*

Molyneux, John (1981) *Leon Trotsky's Theory of Revolution*

Renton, David (2004) *Trotsky.*

Service, Robert. *Trotsky: A Biography*

Stalin: The First In-depth Biography Based on Explosive New Documents from Russia's Secret Archives by Edvard Radzinskii (Paperback - Aug 18, 1997)

Stalin: The Court of the Red Tsar by Simon Sebag Montefiore (Paperback - Sep 13, 2005)

Young Stalin by Simon Sebag Montefiore (Paperback - Oct 14, 2008)

Stalin: Breaker of Nations by Robert Conquest (Paperback - Nov 1, 1992)

Stalin and His Hangmen: The Tyrant and Those Who Killed for Him by Donald Rayfield (Paperback - Dec 13, 2005)

Stalin: Russia's Man of Steel by Albert Marrin (Paperback - Jan 1, 2002)

Stalin in Power: The Revolution from Above, 1928-1941 by Robert C. Tucker (Paperback - Apr 17, 1992)

Hitler and Stalin: Parallel Lives by Alan Bullock (Paperback - Nov 2, 1993)

Printed in Great Britain
by Amazon.co.uk, Ltd.,
Marston Gate.